A Financial Managers Survival Kit

From Survival to Success
in the Financial Services Industry

Library and Archives Canada Cataloguing in Publication

Powell, Greg, 1969-, author
    A financial manager's survival kit : from survival to
success as a sales manager in the financial services industry
/ by Greg Powell, CFP, CHS, EPC, BA (Psych), CD.

Issued in print and electronic formats.
ISBN 978-1-77141-151-6 (paperback).--ISBN 978-1-77141-152-3
(pdf)

    1. Sales force management--Canada. 2. Financial services
industry--Personnel management. I. Title.

HF5439.5.P68 2016   658.85   C2015-908555-1
                                           C2015-908556-X

A Financial Managers Survival Kit

From Survival to Success
in the Financial Services Industry

Greg Powell, CFP, CHS, EPC, BA (psych), CD

First Published in Canada 2016 by Influence Publishing

Book Cover Design: Marla Thompson
Typeset: Greg Salisbury
Proofreader: Sue Kehoe
Portrait Photographer: Carlos Taylhardatj - Art of Headshots

Dedicated to my lovely wife, Julie Cook,
without whom none of this would be possible.

Testimonials

"This book delivers exactly what has been needed for a very long time for the leaders in our industry. Not only does it cover a wide range of subjects, it provides you with the tips to help you better your skills, to implement new ideas and to better achieve your goals."
Shawn Bellefeuille, CFP, CLU, CHS, Desjardins Financial Security Independent Network

"This book is an excellent road map to becoming a successful sales manager. In fact, anyone with aspirations to be a business leader will find several key insights throughout this very relevant book."
Rick Headrick, President, Sun Life Global Investments

"Storytelling and sharing personal experiences is a powerful way to guide new and potential managers through the process from making the career decision to creating success. Greg's willingness and ability to draw not only from his own experience but those of other respected leaders in the financial services and insurance industries provide a solid foundation from which to embark on an exciting journey into sales management."
Karen Watkinson, CHRL, Director, Strategic Initiatives, Sun Life Financial

"Mr. Powell writes for the financial service industry but his principles and concepts apply wherever people lead others in challenging environments. As a regional operations manager I am challenged with acquiring and growing talent at the organizational level and keeping my work and home life balanced. This book informs both well with concise practicality. In the days of O'Leary and Trump it is refreshing to see the path to success in the financial service industry includes community engagement, coaching and mentoring employees, and is compatible with time for family. This book provides practical insight and tools useful to anyone looking to grow their leadership skill."
Keith Shaw B.Sc., Pharm.D. , Regional Pharmacy Manager, Sobeys Inc.

"If you want a career in the Financial Industry, go no further. Mr. Powell in his book brought it all together from the time of entering the business to the time of establishing yourself and arriving at your destination. Background doesn't really matter to be an advisor; most don't even want to consider a career in the insurance sales. Advisors come from all walks of life and they succeed. Management role in the financial industry is perhaps least talked about or appreciated. Their importance is immeasurable. Their role in the advisor's success and the success of the industry is so very important and unrecognised. I predict that the life industry would collapse if there were no managers, all in one generation. No one else would bring them on board. The advisors need a helping hand and field managers understand the concerns an agent goes through. It is best to have this type of person beside you all through your career and life. Thank you Greg for your contributions to our industry and helping us understand the many roles that managers play."
Gopala Alampur, Advisor, Author of *"A Fortune for your Future"*, keynote speaker, 41 year MDRT member

"The Financial Manager's Survival Kit is a must-read for any manager who wants to improve team focus, communication and productivity; a compelling message delivered with insight, and an excellent resource for new and experienced leaders. This is more than a book – it is a compendium with a powerful story, well researched insights, and practical tools. This book delivers!"
Tracey Hansen, FM, A Financial Centre Manager, Sun Life Financial

"Good sales managers, never mind great sales managers, are hard to find. Greg has captured what one that needs to survive and thrive as the result of all the great work we do for clients. Greg's survival handbook is a must read for anyone who wants to not only look at management in the financial services industry but flourish. Why create your own map when one is written for you?"
Rick Frayn CLU, CHS, Financial Centre Manager, Sun Life Financial Hall of Fame 2006

"Greg has done a superb job pulling together the key ingredients for success in building and leading a successful insurance agency. His time spent in the Canadian army infuses the comments and shows how, by keeping the focus on the basics every day, you will achieve success over time: the same formula for success for any new recruit to our industry. His book is both a practical step-by-step guide as well as a source of inspiration for those "down days" we all experience. You and your team will want to keep their own copy of Greg's book handy so they can refer to it regularly."
**David Juvet, LLM, CFP, CLU, CHFC, CHS, FLMI, AMTC
Ideal Solutions Financial Services Inc. Past Chair of The Financial Advisors Association of Canada (TFAAC)**

"Greg Powell has captured the breadth and depth of what it takes to be a successful manager in financial services in the 21st century. His book is a must read for all managers within their first few years of leadership. His insights, along with those of the many contributors, will position you to be a successful leader and to avoid many of the pitfalls that management and leadership can bring. Greg, thank you for your relevant, down to earth practical tips for managers as they face ever changing challenges to the industry."
Greg Pollock, President and CEO, Advocis

"I'm not from the industry and after reading this book I feel like I know what to do to run a branch!"
Elizabeth Jukes, Executive Assistant, Plastics Redeemed

"It is an ideal hand book for the sales manager and agency builder. It has concrete examples and practical field tested ideas of what can be done and how to do it. Insights and material from other professionals rounding out Greg's experience is brilliant. The Financial Managers Survival Kit lives up to its name as it provides an excellent framework for sales managers and agency builders to follow. Weaved through each section are great practical field tested ideas that can be easily adapted to any managers process to bring immediate improved results. The peer contributions add an additional degree of depth to Greg's extensive coverage of the subject."
Tony Bosch, CFP, CLU, CH.F.C, CHS, MFA, Executive Vice President, Broker Development, HUB Financial Inc.

"Greg Powell and his team of proven leadership experts have developed a very field-tested, tactical guide for managers in the financial services space. This book covers many topics that are typically not taught very well in the industry and includes language, processes and techniques used by the best leaders in the business."
Joey Davenport, President, Hoopis Performance Network

"The Financial Manager's Survival Kit" written by Greg Powell should be on the reading list for all new sales managers of financial services agencies. In his book, Powell includes invaluable peer contributions, compensation comparison charts, tips and tactics, extremely well crafted templates. Powell outlines practical ways of recruiting, training, and coaching advisors."
Celia Ciotola, BA, Director of GAMA International Canada and Director Business Development with Advocis ~ The Financial Advisors Association of Canada.

"I have to say this book truly gives us hands-on ideas, they work! I want to input some of these ideas into our branch business plan this year. These are very practical ideas for field managers and in the real world!"
Sonia Wu, Financial Centre Manager, first woman to win the Excellence Cup, Named one of "Top 50 Women of Influence" in the insurance and investment industry in Canada

"The Financial Managers Survival Kit" is an extremely relevant, comprehensive and easy to read compendium of little gems that will not only help new managers to establish a solid foundation for their career... but also, provide veteran managers with great food for thought."
Reid McGruer, B.A.,CFP, CLU, RHU, Ch.F.C.
Regional Director – Freedom 55 Financial

"Finally, a resource for sales managers in the financial services industry! In particular, I appreciated the segment on working with agents of different ages in an intergenerational workforce. This essential resource will surely help managers to accelerate growth and increase success."
Michael Walsh, President, Kaizen Consulting Services Inc. Author of 'Thinking Big is Not Enough: Moving past the myths and misconceptions that stop business growth'.

"A workbook and a guidebook all in one package. Step by step help for managers on their journey to develop themselves as well as advisors and other managers. I love that Greg Powell has drawn on the expertise of so many others as well as his own experiences."
Leslee Lucy, CFP, CPCA, Financial Centre Manager, Sun Life Financial

"The Life Insurance & Financial Planning Industry has always been known as a community of like-minded individuals striving to meet the needs of their clients, companies we represent as well as the public at large. Although the author and contributors may not have crossed each other's paths often or know each other well…it is incredible to see us all come together by collaborating, sharing ideas as well as coveted trade secrets to make our industry better. This book really puts it all together as a coaching tool for managers, trainers and future mentors in our great business."
Alex Chan, CHS, CFP, CPCA, EPC, CFSB, Marketing Director BC, IDC Worldsource Insurance Network

"There are no stars-in-the-eyes promises here. Greg Powell's success is built on logic and hard work, plus a keen sense of people's psychology. Managers in any field could benefit just from his thoughts on retention and the approach to different generations. Like Greg himself, this book is the straight goods without pretence and hype."
Richard Dettman, Business Editor, News 1130

"The Financial Manager's Survival Kit shares proven, field-tested insights on how to recruit, develop and retain top advisors. A must read for any leader serious about succeeding in the financial services industry."
Shawn M. Smith. Vice President, Wealth Management Distribution, Desjardins

"Greg has provided a valuable service to the financial services industry. He has taken the timeless truths of agency building, tested them for today and proven their value for his generation. His tactics demonstrate that battle-tested leaders like him can use the tips and tools of the past to build successful agencies in the future. Congratulations! Read more and build better."
Jim Ruta, Author, Keynote Speaker & Coach, AdvisorCraft Media & Consulting

"Greg's book provides a valuable insight and confirmation that his system works The results speak for themselves. Put this on your agenda as a must read."
Terry Thompson, Financial Centre Manager, Sun Life Financial

"Greg Powell has been a leader in financial services and has given generously of his time and wisdom through involvement with GAMA & Advocis. In this book, Greg adds Thought Leadership to his contributions as a very successful manager & industry leader. Sales managers will benefit from the collective wisdom & insights of Greg & the others who graciously share their experience."
Norm Trainor, Founder, President and CEO of The Covenant Group, keynote speaker and author of "8 Best Practices of High Performing Salespeople"

"Greg Powell has plenty of real world 'boots on the ground' experience, and it shines through in this book. Designed as the comprehensive guide to financial industry management, Greg covers all the key topics, and he also highlights many less known but important factors which lead to management career success. This book will become the foundation of manager training across the financial services industry."
Philip Flostrand, BA (econ), CIM, 25 year veteran Investment Advisor with a major Canadian brokerage firm

"Finally, someone who truly gets the challenges sales managers face: attracting and retaining new advisors. While good recruits are everywhere, Greg Powell shows us how to look at a person's unsung attributes and adversities and inspire success in financial services. A must-read book from someone fully in the management trenches."
Deanne Gage, Editor, FORUM

Acknowledgements

Thank you to my mother, Pat Sieben, who has always shown me the importance of helping others, spotting a phony when you see one, and what a super-human work ethic actually looks like. She gets more done by 9:00 a.m. than most people do in a day. She always supported me no matter what challenge I took on.

Thank you to my father, David Powell, who is the most entrepreneurial man I've ever met and taught me not to apologize to others for being successful. I would not have entered this industry without his dogged determination to open the door.

Thank you to my brothers, Marc and Chris Powell, who are constant beacons of a successful work/life balance and have taught me to not take myself too seriously.

Thank you to my wife, Julie Cook, who has guided and influenced almost every step of my career from advisor to branch manager. From initially recruiting me into the agency many years ago, to teaching me as a rookie manager how to recruit professionally, to making sure I remember what is truly important in life when I come home at the end of each day.

Thank you to Rob Popazzi who has been my mentor, GAMA colleague, and friend over many years. At the time, I didn't always appreciate his "coaching moments" at the time I received them but I'm very thankful for the wisdom now.

Thank you to my managers, resource team, and advisors I have worked with at the Surrey office. I am truly fortunate to work alongside the best in the business. Your dedication and drive to find success by helping others is absolutely admirable and inspires me every day at the branch to be the best I can.

Table of Contents

Introduction - Arriving Back Where I Started

My first awareness of the financial industry starts when I was probably 10 years old.

It was 1979 and my parents had just moved our family from our original home in Delta where I and my two younger brothers had been born. The reason for the big move was largely due to my father transitioning from being an agent with Mutual Life of Canada's New Westminster branch to starting a satellite office in Surrey with a modest handful of agents. With the success of the branch and a new leadership position within a large company, my parents felt it the right time to move our family to a more sizeable home in the White Rock area. This is really when our lifestyle changed. I didn't actually know what my father did for a living other than working in sales, and I thought it had something to do with finance.

I noticed we started enjoying more vacations, the family car parked in our driveway seemed a bit nicer than before, and we all enjoyed a good lifestyle. Afterwards, I became more aware that it was important to be focussed and successful; it gave you options and opportunities many people seem to miss if they just had a "job" versus a career. Many other people in my family's circle were also in the financial industry. Some insurance agents were my Cub Scout leaders, tax specialists and realtors brought their kids over for play-dates, investment advisors invited us to baseball games. I was completely surrounded by people in the industry. Despite the common jokes about insurance salespeople one hears, I personally grew up thinking that these people were the most positive, generous, and ethical individuals on the planet.

When my father's branch would qualify for industry conventions, I would make a little extra money babysitting the children of the other insurance agents while they were having a good time at the gala dinners. Over the years, I developed a little interest in the business but didn't think I had it in me to work in sales.

I specialized in marketing and accounting in high school, I even signed up for the CGA program after high school. On weekends and evenings my father lent me 1980s sales and motivation cassette tapes. He invited me as a young teenager to Achievers International conferences where I heard some of the best inspirational business speakers in the world like Og Mandino and Zig Ziglar. Initially in college, I took accounting and economics courses but found them pretty sterile. I was good at finance and numbers but disliked the lack of human interaction. I found myself gravitating to psychology and sociology. How people behaved and how to influence that behaviour was very intriguing to me.

Around 19 years of age I was attracted to join the army and this was obviously a strange departure from accounting. Further, my family largely had nothing to do with government careers of any kind other than my grandfather who, like many of that generation, had served in World War II. He was an Ordnance Specialist, working with explosives and munitions in the infantry regiments.

One day, two military recruiters showed up at my college campus cafeteria. After some stimulating conversation, I picked up a brochure and showed it to two other friends who were also in similar college studies. They were also intent on doing something completely different. I always thought that it would be interesting after two years of college to take a bit of a break. The military option seemed like a great opportunity for unique and adventurous experiences. So all three of us began the military's selection process and went through interviews, physical exams, and cognitive tests to help place us into suitable military roles. It was suggested that I would be well suited for demolitions and engineering fields.

One rainy day in April 1988 my father dropped me off at the military base parking lot where the buses were lining up to take us to our initial military training. My two friends were nowhere to be seen. I had a choice right there to throw my '80s pink and green neon duffle bag back into the trunk of my dad's Audi or put it into the bus's cargo hold and be taken away. Although my friends weren't there and I would go to boot camp alone, I decided to throw my bag underneath the bus and go find a seat.

I didn't return until after about six months of basic and infantry training. When I did come back, I'm pretty sure everyone would have said I arrived home a bit different from the kid who got on the bus. I won't delve into "war stories" on training, comrades lost along the way, challenges experienced on overseas tours; most wouldn't want to hear about it. However, I will say that the 13 years I spent in the military helped forget who I am today. I had some elements of leadership already but time in the army galvanized me and I truly feel it gave me certain advantages in a management career in the financial industry.

Over the next several years, I learned how to be a combat engineer which involved dealing with explosives, booby-traps, mine warfare (both putting them in the ground and carefully taking them out) as well as building bridges. While we didn't do exactly the same duties, I had a chance to play with the same ordnance my grandfather did, and even train on the same base he did while getting ready for World War II. Our engineer's motto was "first-in, last out" of the battlefield and despite the exhaustive challenges, I loved it. I worked my way up through the rank structure steadily and took on additional roles, signed up for nearly every opportunity that came my way and eventually took the position of the coveted reconnaissance sergeant position.

I completed my university degree in Psychology and Criminology while I was still in the military and graduated from Simon Fraser University in the summer of 2000. Already I was beginning to get itchy feet with my current situation through a combination of frustration with bureaucratic nonsense involving my commanding officer and the constant pressure to keep up with the upcoming young soldiers. More and more often I found myself behind a government-issue desk and less time "doing the job" and getting dirty with the troops.

In May 2001, five months before the tragic 9-11 event, I was already in the process of leaving the military both mentally and physically. Surprisingly, I was introduced to something entrepreneurial; a "dot-com" gift franchise called for some one special.com that a retired army friend was working with. They needed a get-it-done operations director and I had the reputation of problem-solving and getting things done. It was exciting doing something so new and I felt the sky was the limit. I had a taste of running my own schedule versus reporting for duty with someone else's priorities as well getting rewarded for my effort and not just getting paid in my pay scale.

Unfortunately, this was just before the time of the dot-com crash. Online companies like ours started disappearing overnight. Over a quick cup of coffee, I got the news there wasn't a need to come to work the next day. I never once considered going back to the government world or looking for conventional employment. From start to finish, I don't think the whole endeavour lasted a year but it didn't matter; I wanted to find another self-employment role.

Luckily, another opportunity came up rather quickly for an operational director in a similar type of online gift company called web2you.ca. It had survived the dot-com crash better than many other e-commerce shops. While I worked for this company for the next year and a half, I was constantly investigating other fields that would give me limitless opportunities and a chance to expand my leadership skills. My next step would get me closer but I had no idea that I was going to end up in a very familiar place.

In 2002, my father was still in the financial services industry but Mutual Life of Canada had changed its name to Clarica. He had been working on starting a business called Strategic Management Consultants. SMC was going to provide aptitude profiling, training, and consulting to a wide range of sales companies. I worked with him closely in this ambitious project for many months and eventually it came time for me to dedicate to it full-time and become President of SMC.

Along the way, we developed an international speaker's bureau and collected some of the best people in their fields, people that audiences would pay good money to hear; from a high-end tailor who made suits for the gangster Al Capone, a media business anchorman, gold-medal Olympian to adventurers who climbed Mount Everest and visited both poles. From something that started so small, we ended up expanding across Canada, the US, and even into Australia. I got a taste of public speaking while working alongside top salespeople in diverse industries and found myself rubbing shoulders with some of the best entrepreneurs and self-made professionals on the planet. It was like throwing gas on a flame.

While our international company was doing well and actually going in the right career direction for me, it wasn't something I saw myself necessarily doing long term. In 2004, my father, who had remained part of Clarica as a manager at the Vancouver agency at the time, encouraged me to try an aptitude test for the financial services industry. I reluctantly did it and although I never saw the results until much later, he told me that I "passed." It took some convincing on his part to make me think I had any sales DNA but I went through the selection steps cautiously, still not really sure if this was the journey that was meant for me. I eventually signed up for the life license course while I continued to look at other career options.

I got through the insurance licensing process quickly and completed the market identification booklet as all of us do. Most of my progression was done off-the-record as I hadn't interviewed with the company's recruiting manager yet, just my father so far and that was pretty informal. In the fall of 2003, I met the manager for Clarica's Abbotsford agency and we discussed an advisor-to-manager fast-track program. I agreed to be an advisor initially to attain certain achievements, learn the products and sales processes, and earn some credibility in this industry before trying on a leadership role.

A series of events led to a decision not to pursue the role at this agency as originally discussed. However, later that same week, I received a phone call from the branch manager of the Surrey Clarica office who was willing to pick up where I had left off with the Abbotsford office. The irony wasn't lost on me; the same agency that my father had founded in Surrey 30 years ago and that was such a big part of my upbringing would be my doorstep to a new career.

The Surrey branch manager wanted to meet with me for lunch to discuss timelines and expectations. Our second meeting included the regional manager to finalize details of my six months proving period: complete 25 insurance sales within three months, qualify for a sales campaign, get my additional wealth and trade approver licenses completed, and bring in one new recruit to the agency. Successful completion of this meant I would be accepted to Clarica's Manager Training Program (MTP). Oddly, this wasn't the hard part of getting into the Surrey agency; my biggest challenge would prove to be the winning over of Julie Cook, the recruiting manager.

Julie was a very successful recruiting manager. But having been brought up in a Mennonite community that abhors fighting of any kind, she was also a conscientious objector. These philosophies and beliefs didn't blend well with my background as a soldier. Our first meeting took over two hours but I guess I eventually must have done well because not only did she approve of me joining the branch as an agent and later a manager colleague but several years later we got married!

While completing my pre-management requirements I groomed myself for the role. I picked up the other licenses quickly and voraciously learned our compensation system and product lines. It was stimulating, gave me a better income than army pay and lots of time flexibility, as well as provided the professional development I craved. Over the next four and a half years, I worked through various management roles in the company, learned from some of the best managers in the business, and received my Certified Financial Planner (CFP) designation amongst others.

After the name change from Clarica to Sun Life Financial in 2008, I knew I was eventually going to leave the Regional Manager role despite enjoying this position very much. Julie and I looked at branches that I could return to as a manager. We looked all over the country but again fate seemed to have a plan for me. I eventually accepted an agency leadership position back at the Surrey office. At that time, there were 28 agents in that branch but we both knew it had huge potential amongst a growing suburban geographic area that I intimately knew.

It must have been a good choice. Our agency has almost doubled the numbers of agents and managers as well as our agency revenues and it recently received one of the highest distinctions that can be awarded in our company called President's Circle. This measures consistent sales production, agent quality, and recruiting growth. It is one of the highlights of my working career. Not too shabby for a guy that wanted nothing to do with insurance or sales. Looking back it was a strange winding path that led me again to the halls of the insurance office that I roamed when I was in grade 6. Currently I sit in the chair that was used not only by my father but also by my wife when she was branch manager. I doubt that has been done too many times in our company or our industry. The funny part is that now my father asks for more career updates than my VP and the lady I go home to every night has a detailed knowledge of how convention and recruiting metrics work. Both had a large impact on creating the agency and culture I now lead.

No pressure…

Peer Contributors – Wisdom from the Field

To add to the kaleidoscope of my personal points of view and professional commentary on subject matter in this book, I wanted to include some of the great peers I've been fortunate to work with over the years. They are agency managers, business coaches, and experienced field leaders who have found success within the sales and the financial services industry. Together they represent a wide range of skills from the investment, banking, insurance, and estate planning worlds as well as come from diverse company models including independent brokers, career agency, and franchised business models.

Most importantly, of course, is these particular leaders are willing to share their ideas with fellow peers and new managers in an effort to give people the best chance to move from survival to success in a demanding performance-based career. In a highly competitive world, this access to expertise is coveted.

The topics they will address are those that are often front of mind for any new or developing manager in our field such as tips for career longevity, building agency culture, priority management, communication, leveraging resources, and avoiding pitfalls. Rather than just having my perspective on these points, you will have access to a dozen.

Their wisdom will enhance and add colour to the often "black and white lines" of the pictures we will be working on in this book. I greatly appreciate their knowledge and give my heartfelt thanks to their willingness to share. A great mentor once told me "A rising tide raises all boats" and I believe it. By keeping people around us that are smarter, faster, and stronger than we are now allows us to keep growing and perfecting our craft.

My sincerest gratitude to each of you,

Greg Powell

Alphabetically by last name:

Andrew Barber-Starkey, Master Certified Coach, President and Founder Procoach Success System, North Vancouver, BC andrew@procoachsystem.com

Shawn Bellefeuille, CFP, CLU, CHS Desjardins Financial Security Independent Network Ottawa, ON shawn.bellefeuille@dfsinottawa.ca

Tony Bosch, CFP, CLU, CH.F.C., CHS, MFA, BA Executive Vice President, Broker Development at HUB Financial Inc. Vancouver, BC tony.bosch@hubfinancial.com

Alex Chan, CHS, CFP, CPCA, EPC, CFSB Marketing Director of IDC Worldsource Insurance Langley, BC alex.chan@idcwin.ca

Julie Cook, FLMI, EPC President of Upstage, 25 years with Mutual Life, Clarica and Sun Life Financial
Chilliwack, BC   Julie@upstagenow.ca

Tony Defazio, CPCA, RHU 27 year Agent with Mutual Life, Clarica and Sun Life Financial
Maple Ridge, BC Tdefazio@telus.net

Neil Hanson, CFP, CLU, CH.F.C. CPCA 25 year field manager and large-case coach
Victoria, BC neilhanson@shaw.ca

Izumi McGruer, CFP, CLU, CH.F.C., CHS Director, Regional Manager, Freedom 55 Financial, Vancouver, BC I.MikiMcGruer@freedom55financial.com

 **Warren Miles-Pickup,** BA, Director of Wealth Sales, SLGI
Vancouver, BC warren.s.miles.pickup@sunlife.com

 **Robert Popazzi**, BA, CLU, CHS, AVP Sales Force Growth and Development Sun Life Financial
Kitchener, ON Robert.popazzi@sunlife.com

 **Robin Rankine**, CLU, ChFC, CLU, Financial Centre Manager,
Edmonton, AB Robin.rankine@sunlife.com

Section 1

Know Where You Are to Know Where You Are Going

Setting the Stage

Why is this book needed?

That's simple; there are almost no books addressing key skills for sales managers in the financial industry. I know because I desperately looked during my initial and formative years as a new manager. Moreover, they aren't future-facing and therefore don't address the challenges we are going to have in the upcoming decades. This is where this book fits on your shelf.

I often reflect back to my first year as a sales manager. Over my rookie year I learned from many different and often conflicting sources. I greedily assimilated as much of this material as I could pick up online, at bookstores, at management conferences, and at industry trade shows. Looking back over a dozen years I was never able to find a single "starting out" sales management guidebook or a collection of good tips and essential skills that I could implement. It is my hope that this book will fill this gap and give junior managers, or those looking to become managers, a fighting chance.

A developing manager may need to learn or step up to different parts of the job at varying times in their career. Likely you don't plan to be in the same chair you are today and have aspirations for the future! Perhaps initially you might come into an agency as a trainer, then later move into a recruiting role then change into a marketing position or launch a satellite office. From time to time, we'd all like to have reference materials on our desks to pick up when needed and quickly flip to the relevant chapter. This book gives easy to follow, scalable methods to use immediately for creating a recruiting plan, penetrating different markets, ways of training new recruits, developing and communicating a recognition system, and building a sales campaign culture.

We all pick up ideas and tools over many years, and we get stronger and more fluid in our craft as time passes. Eventually you will obtain a personal career toolbox sufficient to get through most challenges. Trust me, it will happen. You will sound like those senior managers and leaders who have the perfect way of smoothly handling any retention issue or create a last-minute recruiting strategy without skipping a beat. When you are first in the business you hear of managers who are 10 or 20 years in the game and you are just in awe of how much there is simply in their head. You dream about connecting to them with a USB cable to download their how-to files. All it takes is time. You just need to survive long enough in the agency to build your own toolbox. Therein lies the problem.

Here is a familiar scenario: you are a new sales manager typically functioning in a training role. You pick up your phone one morning and hear a panicked call from a colleague, "I'm stuck in traffic and can't make it for my two o'clock recruiting appointment with Ted. Can you please meet Ted and get him signed up for his licensing course?" Normally that situation would cause someone considerable stress if they're not familiar with the objectives of a recruiting meeting or the steps involved to move the candidate forward in the selection process. A reference book like this allows you to flip to that respective chapter and run a complete interview and cover the main points, moving the candidate to the next step. Later that day you would be able to tell your colleague proudly that you were able to handle it.

Like a well-worn cookbook, if you need to bake cookies you don't have to recall how to from a long-ago course taken. You simply open the book, pick out the cookies you want to bake, and follow the instructions!

When I look at our industry, we tend to pick things up from one another at LAMP conferences once a year or leaning on a colleague's doorframe in the afternoon picking their brains on particular topics. We often collect and trade tips, tools, and documents. This works most of the time, but you have to come to the conference or have competent colleagues who have an open-door policy.

Having this how-to book should reinforce the teachings of most head offices in the industry, not contradict them. It will also have a collection of best practises from some amazing field managers who come from a large array of companies providing a talented spectrum of topics. They provide a more complete base of knowledge than any one single company or model can possess. At your fingertips, you have the insights of a dozen successful managers from a variety of companies that encompass tens of thousands of advisors and thousands of field managers whose agencies go from ten handpicked agents in a boutique fee-for-service model to thousands of advisors flying under one banner.

Common conversations arise at National Advocis and NAIFA meetings as well as international financial industry conferences like LAMP and MDRT where diverse agents and managers come together. Common questions always come up. How do you find enough high-quality prospects while running your own business? How do you slow down the revolving door of retention with the competition for talent that lies ahead in future year? How do you run effective interview meetings in less than 30 minutes? How do you identify, penetrate and recruit in new markets? How do you increase attendance for development training and even leverage it to keep your agents longer? How can you pull everyone together with a cohesive agency culture and impactful communication strategies?

There are online courses on subjects such as recruiting or retention for a price tag of $200 to $500, and for much bigger invoices and travel costs, you can attend multi-day workshops to develop and strengthen needed skills. However, the advantage of a quick reference book is that it's always there and can provide instant guidance if suddenly your role changes at the agency and you become in charge of recruiting or retention tomorrow. This book will help you survive and thrive in a challenging career.

In the upcoming industry landscape, a book like this is incredibly needed. Certainly the hunt for talent, and of course the retention of that talent, will be even more difficult in the next few decades. Baby boomers are leaving their careers and the Generation X and Generation Y populations have much smaller numbers to fill the ranks. There will be fierce competition indeed attracting the people needed to service our clientele. Only those agents who are prepared to act and cross-train themselves quickly to develop an adequate point of reference will survive. In this career, it normally takes five years to become competent in the needed sales and financial skill sets.

With the industry's experience heading out the door towards retirement not every new manager will have a great mentor nor be given hundreds of thousands of dollars worth of training. What is in your hands now are the essential points and strategies to be successful in a financial sales management career. It is a culmination of the best practises, ideas, and outlooks from world-class managers from a wide range of models, which I have learned from. Even if your particular situation or agency environment is a little bit different than what is described within the pages of this book, the core strategies and concepts will guide you most of the way through the challenges you will experience.

The more I investigated the matter the more I was stunned to discover the absence of a comprehensive book that a sales organization in our industry could give their new and developing field managers. Over the year and a half I worked on this project, I focussed on making this book fill that gap for our profession. It is my dream that this book is on every new sales manager's desk.

A great mentor of mine said to me once, "A rising tide raises all boats." Every time one of us shares knowledge or spends time with someone at the early stages of learning their careers, we raise the tide a little bit and we are all the better for it. At the end of the day what will matter most is not what you got, but what you gave; not what you learned, but what you taught; not your accomplishments, but your impact on others; and not your own memories, but what people remember you for.

Managers are Essential

Most North Americans are going to live at least 25 to 30 years in retirement. The two biggest driving factors from a client's perspective are: I'd like to have an active and healthy life as long as possible, but I don't want to outlive my assets. I don't want to be alive and broke. It may be hard to hear but money and health will largely dictate the happiness and comfort level we all experience in our retirement, which can essentially be a third of our lifespan.

Having the most current cellphone or having a fast motorcycle is not going to be as important as being able to travel to see the grandkids, buy healthy groceries, and the ability to afford hearing aids, good medicine, at-home nursing, and physiotherapy. These "luxuries" come with that lifestyle but they have a price tag that unfortunately not everybody in our country is able to pay.

We are fortunate with the medical industry in Canada where so much of our federal and provincial system provides basic medical care for its citizens. However, there is not much out there other than Social Security or Canadian Pension Plan (CPP) that provides basic financial care. And while it's better than a slap in the face, giving somebody less than a thousand dollars a month (that's pre-tax too) to deal with the cost of living in 2016 won't amount to much. It's hardly enough to live on let alone enjoy during retirement.

So it's incredibly important that everyone in our financial industry does their job well; I would say it's as important as medical doctors doing their job well. There are recruiters in campuses encouraging people to join medical and law schools and there is already large competition to be in these white-collar careers. But there are recruiters out there for the financial industry too, that's not an accident.

There are not a lot of professional recruiters being paid very good incomes to prospect candidates, filter resumes, and build referral networks to find the next person to stand in a coloured vest in front of a retail super-mart greeting people as they walk in. Why? Because the people staffing those jobs are easy to find and, more importantly, they're remarkably easy to replace.

However, the financial industry takes time to "grow" good financial advisors and they are serving an incredibly important job in our society. Managers need to know how to find agents, train them, get them self-sufficient quickly, and run a business practise in an ethical manner. Then after all that, maintain these agents for decades until they retire. No small feat.

There is currently no comprehensive aide-memoire book for field managers in the Canadian financial industry. Some e-books and booklets on isolated topics exist on the internet. They seem to only speak with the voice of one organizational model (like a franchise or bank model) but I could not find a multi-disciplinary book that simply wanted to help me with the day-to-day struggles I and my colleagues encountered in the initial years.

While the "feel" of this book is largely for career agency models, the challenges are similar for independent channels too. We are all experiencing the challenges of our roles regardless of the logos on our business cards. I believe that following systems developed by some of the top peers in our industry will help not only the survival of new managers entering the role but the industry at large going into challenging decades ahead.

This book is organized and written in a common language that sales managers, leaders, and professionals in the financial industry currently use. No matter what company we belong to we are part of a larger industry, and we face similar challenges every day.

Primarily this book will be targeted to "junior" field managers (which I define as less than five years in the business) in agency systems or independent MGA models, head office executives, and advisors. This book will cover topics and techniques that financial services managers around the world can use but it will be focussed on the North American landscape. It is an ideal resource for:

- current sales managers looking for an edge on the local competition or their peers in the hallways.
- ambitious new branch managers who want to succeed in a role where you can't make too many mistakes while simultaneously learning how to build a productive field force and juggling the many balls of leadership.
- a head office training tool for managers in new roles such as newly

promoted managers from either within the agency ranks or from management outside the financial industry

- a new manager of a Managed General Agency (MGA) or any other sales-based group like mortgage brokers or general insurance agencies.
- a "clean slate" opportunity such as an opening in new geographic location or starting a new management team paradigm.
- existing agencies looking to expand the sales power of their own business model.
- senior agents desiring a new prodigy to mentor, planning a replacement of a manager on their team, or even looking for a successor to take on the family business.

By reading this book, I want the reader to gain practical knowledge they can apply immediately that will have both a short-term and long-term impact on their careers. The book will give concrete examples, descriptive demonstrations, quick application ideas, and comprehensive scripting on the critical parts of our roles. In addition to specific takeaways, it will provide some philosophical elements to enjoy long-term satisfaction and success in a difficult career path. The reader can keep the book as a future quick-reference tool as their careers develop and new responsibilities are taken on.

By following a logical path, this book is both realistic and often inspirational in outlining how to be successful at different stages of the lifecycles of both a sales manager and an agency—from the vision of what you are trying to build, selecting the right people, producing recognition campaigns, to succession planning at the end of an agent's or a manager's career.

It concerns me how many individuals attempt a career in financial services management only to not make it beyond the first year. Manager candidates, whether from outside industries or even successful agents from within our organizations' ranks, deserve the best chance to thrive and make an impact. While not everyone will enjoy a career in sales management, I do not want to see any more with great potential fail simply because they didn't have some kind of map to get through the darker parts of the forest.

We are the "sales force" of our profession and without our success there will be no industry to provide financial planning to the North American population. I can't stress this enough. Sales managers equal the future of our industry; without us, there will be no agents, no agencies and therefore businesses and families will not get that all-important assistance in financial planning that could lead to disaster in the future.

It is my hope this book will be a resource and how-to book for the key activities of financial sales management in North America of not only core accountabilities such as recruiting, development, and retention of financial agents but also how to create and develop a winning agency or branch.

Create a Vision

By chance, it is the beginning of a New Year as I work on this piece so it seems an appropriate time to discuss vision and goal setting. Vision is what you want to build, it's the ideals and principles you want to implement, the dream you have for your office. It's important to understand there is a difference between vision and strategy. Vision is the ideal, hoped-for, glass brimming over full idea for your office.

Without a vision, your strategy will have no roots to grow from, no aspiration. Vision is the magnet that pulls you forward through days, months, and years. It keeps you focussed and moving despite distractions and detractors. If the magnet has a big enough magnetic field it will pull those around you too.

Visioning is a process, not an output, and needs to be inclusive. It involves gathering information from those around you about what's important to them and aligning it with what's important to you. Once you share your vision with people, it needs to be accompanied by the caveat that it will be reviewed regularly for relevance and the request, "Please share your thoughts, because we are always open to new perspectives and other ways of thinking about our future." That approach will make the vision more meaningful and resilient.

I recommend that before you read the next section you know what your vision is for your agency. These are some of the questions you need to answer for yourself as a leader and perhaps it would not be a poor idea to have other sales managers in your team answer them too:

a. What's important to me?
b. What will I not compromise on?
c. What are my core beliefs?
d. What excites me about the future? Hopes, dreams, predictions?
e. How much time will I give myself to achieve this vision?
f. How will I know I've made it?
g. If I had a genie bottle, what would my three wishes for my agency be?
   1. _____
   2. _____
   3. _____

MY AGENCY VISION IS:

_____

_____

Now that you have the basis of your vision, the next step is figuring out the goals that move your office in the direction of that vision. Take the vision and determine the tangible actions that would need to occur. Work the tangibles backwards from the long-range goal to the digestible bits.

For example, let us say your vision is to have a large office with only contributing, engaged advisors who are full-time financial professionals. Sounds simple but what does that mean? Make that specific. What is a large agency to you or your organization: fifty, one hundred, or five hundred agents? What is a contributing, engaged advisor? Does it mean MDRT qualification, six-figure income, client retention numbers, a certain client block size? Lastly, what do you mean by a financial professional? Answers could range from being a full-time agent with high school equivalency to a multiply-licensed Certified Financial Planner (CFP).

Answer the questions to each element of your vision, working to a place where you have specific numbers for each piece. Be as granular as you can, then you will have specific goals to focus on. Like a financial plan, it needs to be monitored and updated regularly. The vision or goals you have in your first year as a leader may not be relevant five years later. Identify what each goal looks like at the end of the year. Break down this goal into quarterly, monthly, and even weekly objectives. Now the path ahead of you may seem a bit clearer and more manageable.

Do not wait until you have a perfect map worked out, start walking in the direction you know you want to head and make adjustments as you journey towards your vision. Too often people procrastinate or delay moving forward because they feel they haven't worked out 100 percent of the details. You know which mountain you want to climb to the top of, you will find the best path to get there as you journey.

Why Should Someone Join the Financial Services Industry?"

You and I belong to one of the most important industries in the world.

What actually is the opportunity in the financial service industry over the next 20 years? Well, I don't have a crystal ball but just watching how things have shifted even in the last dozen years in which I have been directly involved I see huge opportunities in many industries such as telecommunications, health care, energy and resources, technology, and some others. But let's focus on our industry going forward and review some numbers on this one.

Within the next 20 years, the parents of the baby boomers will be gone. These parents are now currently in their seventies and eighties and they're hanging on to considerable cash amounts, property assets, investments, and recreational properties. The baby boomers are going to be receiving all of that wealth. So let us go forward 10 years—the boomers themselves are going to be where their parents are right now, and that's a problem. They will be holding the accumulated wealth of their own and their parent's along with the tax, probate, and family headaches that will go with it. These people are going to need help and advice.

With medical advancements, early detection of diseases, and better nutritional access, the boomers are probably going to achieve the age of one hundred years. So let's assume they retire at age 65; that's 30-35 years of retirement! Even during this retirement period they are going to be gaining assets, using those assets (hopefully in a tax efficient manner) and in some case passing on their assets to the next generation.

Over the next 20 years these boomers, when this cohort wants to (some will have this choice but some unfortunately won't), are going to pass on their companies, assets, and property to the next generation. As an industry, we have been talking about this massive, unprecedented, inter-generational wealth transfer for years now, and the media certainly bangs the drums loudly on this topic too, but I don't see agencies doing anything substantially different in their practises. People need to be ready for the storm that's coming, and we are the professionals that are going to be needed more than ever before to help.

For many of this retiring population the changes will be gradual but for some it will be cataclysmic and the financial services industry will be essential. You couldn't have picked a better industry to represent, and I hope you're taking your vitamins because we are going to be very busy in the next couple of decades. The opportunities for investment wealth transfers, coordinating benefits for health care, handling insurance death claims, changing market-based assets into guaranteed income streams, and people needing to make their own pensions (because they didn't have a gold-plated defined benefit pension like their grandparents did) and so on will be staggering. These people will have assets, but most don't know how to make sense of what to do with them.

Like a kid who found their dad's gun, someone may get hurt if they are not careful...

Succession planning

Think about it, most advisors have client blocks of business that are plus or minus ten years their own age. This is natural because most agents network and interact with other people with similar backgrounds and experiences. For example, a 40-year-old advisor will have a client block of business that will largely be somewhere between 30 and 50 years old. That's where they're more comfortable to prospect and serve, and where the clients are more prone to trust and desire working with the agent. If that is where their markets are then that is where their referrals are.

It is also where their immediate community is generally based from too; friends, business owners, and so on. So from a succession-planning point of view, agents tend to leave behind a client block of business that, more or less, reflects their own background and age. The baby boomers have built one of the biggest business blocks and networks we may ever see in North America. When they eventually leave the workforce, and we aren't going to be able to coerce them to stay forever, they will need to pass their businesses down to the next generation of advisors to service.

We are fortunate enough that this industry does not force people out of their careers at age 65. An agent can do this job; hey, you can have this career until you're 90 if you're fit and have the inclination. No one is going to say you can't do the job, as long as you're mentally able and physically able to do the role. In our roles as agents and managers, they pay us for our problem-solving brains and social personalities, not our physical capabilities. You've got a job for life if that's what you want to do.

However, eventually even the most enthusiastic member of our industry will have their priorities change and then there will be hundreds if not thousands of clients, and business practises that will be generating lots of revenue money. Some businesses may be sold for the equity that has been built or perhaps simply because the senior advisor leaves the clients to a younger custodian to take care of.

Now because the client block is like themselves, when an advisor retires at age 65 their clients will likely be around 55 to 75 years old and will probably live and survive (just like the former advisor) for another quarter century. So more than ever successors need to be found, trained, and kept in our industry until they get tapped on the shoulder for the business opportunity of the century.

The financial services companies that work in insurance will, as long as the premiums are paid, make sure that the insurance that was put in place for the client many years ago will pay out to their beneficiaries. It is the financial companies that manufacture the products, not the agent selling them, that maintain these products long term. This is a good thing; it assures the products and services will be in place long after the client signs the application form. This is even more the case with investments that need constant adjustment and vigilance. In fact, the agent may be retired, or has even passed on, before their client's products pay out. I find it ironic when agents argue over "their" clients like they actually own or possess them. It's like two birds sitting on top of an elephant arguing which bird own the animal they are riding.

That is both the point and the opportunity for the next generation. Clients still have to be maintained by someone representing the company, their products and services need to be monitored and updated: beneficiaries change, risk tolerances change, markets and economies change, and life objectives change (e.g. from a children's education fund to retirement planning to preserving health to estate planning). That is just a taste of the variables the client brings to the table. From an industry perspective, insurance and investment products often change with a "shelf life" of 3-5 years. The advisors who put financial solutions into place may not still be in the role at the critical time to ensure all these transitions happen as planned. They are going to need a successor.

The opportunity for agents now in their thirties or forties is breathtaking; just take a look at the senior blocks of business out there. They can have their choice of who to mentor under and be part of a succession plan. It's going to be a buyer's market in the next few decades and it is one of the hottest and most practical times in history to accumulate large client blocks as part of an agent's business plan. That idea would have been laughable just a few years ago. There may not be as much competition as one may suspect either; the succeeding workforce is going to be much smaller than the departing baby-boomer workforce.

While we're at it let's talk about block sizes too. Successful agents who may be used to having 800 to 1,500 clients to service and be responsible for may soon have to deal with 2,000 to 3,000 clients to maintain in the next 20 years. That may be the new "normal" for our industry, that's why it's imperative we find good agents, develop them for the storm that lies ahead, hire the needed assistants, get the systems in place, and most importantly keep them long enough to be there to pick up the pieces once the biggest workforce shift in history happens.

Do the math: It's not possible to do what we've done before. Most of us only have 250 workdays in a year after taking off weekends and some holidays. If you have 1,000 clients then you would need to see 4 of them each day just to see each client only once a year. Wow. That doesn't leave us much time to grow our business. But what if that number doubled?

We will all have to think differently in the future. Agents and managers will have to leverage systems and technology like Skype simply to be able to keep in touch with clients and the sales force without spending time on the road. The volume of clients they will be serving is going to be massive. And remember, managers are the sales force of our industry. Without their influence, there would be virtually no advisors in our country. Nobody gets out of high school and says, "thank goodness I finished my last exams today. I've been dying to be an insurance agent." That doesn't happen because they're still dreaming about being firefighters, police officers, or like myself they go and join the army.

Very few people seek out the financial services industry as their first career choice. Some agents are lucky and have their sons or daughters follow in their footsteps but this doesn't happen as much as we want it to. Managers need to find these agents for without them the industry as we know it will stop. Like a train that loses its locomotive engine, it will keep moving along the track for a while simply with the inertia that exists within the machine. It will coast along for a while but it will gradually slow down and eventually, one day, simply stop.

More often than not, recruits that we prospect usually do about 10 to 15 years of bouncing around in the workforce trying different occupations. Maybe some go to university, or get married, or get a mortgage, or get their first termination slip or divorce papers before they decide to try something different. They then have a better feeling for what they like and they don't like in a career. These are the "influence-able" people that need to be educated about our career. Even if they decide the career is not for them, they are often grateful for learning more about it and appreciate the impact of what we do for a living.

Certainly, the teachers and faculty in universities and high schools are not promoting our opportunity at their career fairs. It goes against their thinking to say "Hi Tommy, now that you've graduated why not look at being self-employed." It will never happen. Most "institutionalized" workers like schoolteachers, retail employees, and government employees are often terrified to be self-employed. Other professionals such as specialist doctors, lawyers, and business owners understand that to have a chance to really prosper in an occupation you need to run your own ship.

Do the math: It's not possible to do what we've done before. Most of us only have 250 work days in a year after taking off weekends and some holidays. If you have 1,000 clients then you would need to see 4 of them each day just to see each client only once a year. Wow. That doesn't leave us much time to grow our business, but what if that number doubled.

We will all have to think differently in the future. Agents and managers will have to leverage systems and technology like Skype simply to be able keep in touch with clients and the sales force without spending time on the road. The volume of clients they will be serving is going to be massive. And remember managers are the sales force for our industry. Without their influence, there would virtually no advisors in our country. Nobody gets out of high school and says "thank goodness I finished my last exams today. I've been dying to be an insurance agent". That doesn't happen because they're still dreaming about being firefighters, police officers, or like myself goes and join the army.

Very few people as their first career choice seek out of financial services industry. Some agents are lucky and have their sons or daughters follow in the footsteps but this doesn`t happen as much as we want it to. Managers need to find them, without them the industry, as we know it will stop. Like a train that loses its locomotive engine, it will keep moving along the track for a while simply with the inertia that exists within the machine. It would coast along for a while but it would gradually slow down and eventually, one day, simply stop.

More often than not, recruits that we prospect usually do about 10 to15 years of bouncing around in the workforce trying different occupations. Maybe some go to university, get married and a mortgage, getting their first termination slip or divorce papers before they decide to try something different. They have a better feeling for what they like and they don't like in a career. These are the influence-able people that needed to be educated about our career. Even if they decide the career is not for them they are often grateful for learning more about it and appreciate the impact of what we do for a living.

Certainly the teachers and faculty in universities and high schools are not promoting our opportunity at their career fairs. It goes against their thinking to say "Hi Tommy, now that you've graduated why not look at being self-employed". It will never happen. Most 'institutionalized' workers like school teachers, retail employees and government members are often terrified to be self-employed;. Other professionals such as specialist doctors, lawyers and business owners understand that to have a chance to really prosper in an occupation you need to run your own ship.

Importance of Building a Manager Bench

The problem continues within the manager ranks as well. Since there is going to be less of a workforce pool to pick advisors from there is obviously going to be a smaller pool to find good managers from too. As I mentioned before, advisors themselves are going to have to deal with larger blocks, more complex systems and compliance rules alongside growingly sophisticated products because that's what the large demographic is going to demand. Therefore, we need even better managers today tackling more challenges than ever before.

Like agents, managers will have to do more with less people and an ever-increasing complicated environment. My father, a successful 30-year veteran manager of this industry looks at what I have to do now in agency management and shakes his head. He doesn't know how I juggle it all and not go insane.

Those who are interested (for the right reasons) and possess the DNA to be successful field managers are going to be in high demand. This is simply because nothing happens without recruiters and sales managers in our industry. Every once in a while a senior advisor will find a potential candidate but their actual job is sales and taking care of clients, and not recruiting, training, coaching, and administrating over rookies every day. Agents are trying to run their own business, not do your job at the same time. If this industry sustains and, ideally, grows in the decades ahead it will be because of leaders such as you holding this book.

Managers that are dedicated to growing and supporting a strong field force will always be in demand. No matter what happens in the changing financial industry's landscape you will always be in demand. We are an essential service to the people in our world no different than tradespeople, doctors, and farmers. You will never see universities, legal offices, or hospitals disappear from our communities; those institutions are needed. Similarly, the institutions for field management in the financial industry are always going to be required.

There are two things human beings care about most: living a healthy high-quality life as long as possible, and being able to have the finances in place to provide options and to be able to enjoy that life as long as possible.

What we do is extremely important. You are needed, you are essential.

Combat Leadership for Sales Management

I often think there are great parallels between the financial industry and the military. As a former decorated military soldier and now a branch manager within our profession I'm in a somewhat unique position to make that observation.

Soldiers and advisors put themselves in harm's way every day. Advisors prospect by phone (many would rather be shot at!), ask tough personal medical and financial questions, and ask people over their dining room tables to face their mortality and morbidity. Not a fun Friday night in most people books.

However, we've accepted this challenge because we believe we can make a difference in people's lives. I've always said those who can't pass the doctor's physical for the army should look at this career, it's the hardest job you'll ever do or love. The rewards are tremendous but it's not an easy career. Leaders are needed.

The Army was my career before I retired after 13 years and joined the financial services industry. It gave me the opportunity to continue to serve others and have a meaningful impact on their lives. It has proven every bit as challenging and rewarding as my military career, but I'm not often shot at and I don't have to wear the exact same thing ... every ... single ... day!

Many people wouldn't draw a parallel between a professional soldier and a leader in the financial industry but the principles of the Combat Leadership Course (CLC) taught to leaders of the Armed Forces shows the parallels to our industry quite clearly. Soldiers showing aptitude in leadership are invited to take a Combat Leadership Course; one of the most punishing and rewarding programs I've experienced. We are taught ten battle-proven principles of leadership and given opportunities to demonstrate our understanding in real-life situations.

Clients are not feeling fear and confusion because of bullets flying, rockets or bombs exploding, but they're certainly feeling it as a result of investment market scares, uncertainty in the housing markets, and apprehension about the future if there was a severe and prolonged interruption in their ability to generate income for their families. With that type of mayhem out there leadership is paramount

Soldiers participating in combat leadership courses are taught ten principles of leadership. We'll explore each of those principles that I followed while leading soldiers in my platoon, and now apply within my agency as well.

Principle #1: Develop Leadership Potential Within Your Team

You have a mission for your agency or business—for the year, the quarter, or the campaign. But if something changes, and it invariably does, the mission still needs to be accomplished. Be sure you have a team that is capable of taking the mission to completion regardless of unexpected ambushes, calculated losses, and enemy attacks. That means developing the potential within your team. So be attentive to those around you that exhibit leadership potential.

Provide members of your team with the opportunity to seek out and accept responsibility. You can do this by delegating tasks and projects. Coach them and provide feedback as they perform; allow them the chance to fail. You can be the role model for the behaviour you wish to see in these potential leaders. And when they successfully handle the responsibilities you gave them, give them more.

This applies particularly to those colleagues who you suspect may even be stronger than you in certain skills. Don't let ego or your personal ambitions get in the way of letting another perform to their ability; instead, be proud you discovered and developed a talented person. Do anything less and you will compromise the mission.

Principle #2: Know Your People and Promote Their Welfare.

Before I'd ask a soldier to run 20 kilometres cross-country carrying a heavy rucksack I would first need to know his fitness level. In our industry, it's important to know our advisors strengths, abilities, ambitions, background, education, and lifestyle so you can adequately provide them with training and opportunities that will complement these elements. Work on business relationships with each person in the entire team, not only the ones you naturally gravitate to. If you believe a member of your team has potential not yet developed, seek ways to provide that individual the chance to experiment with it.

Once we've identified areas to develop in our people, we train them, hard. Challenge and prepare them for the hardship they will face so that they can endure it and conquer it. This takes the form of teaching scripts, practicing techniques, conducting role-plays, and enlisting them in professional courses.

Soldiers are drilled over and over in battle procedures until it becomes natural and automatic. Similarly, our teams should be drilled in the survival skills of referral talks, closing, prospecting, and handling objections. Once they have mastered the basics, increase the standards and professionalism in which these skills are executed. Create realistic and challenging training that requires the team to work together successfully.

Principle #3: Be a Team

A soldier is dependent on his unit's abilities, strength, and support for his very life. Although our lives are not dependent on one another's to that dramatic extent, we can certainly accomplish more of our business mission when we rely on one another for assistance.

When our mission is unfolding exactly as planned and the sniper is still hidden in the bush, each person can feel confident that the job will get done. However, when the orange bullet tracers light up the night sky and the ambush has begun, we need to link arms and get through the night together. Remember you are setting them out to do a hard job where many do not survive. The team that will achieve its mission objective with the most success and least losses is the team whose arms are linked tightest.

Communicate the end-state of the mission, we call this the "Commander's

Intent," to every member of the team. Each person has to know the goal to be achieved; the team has to have "one mind." Set and accept only high standards from your team. When your Commanding Officer comes by the office, boast about the team's achievement, not your own.

Principle #4: Seek and Accept Responsibility

Looking down at your toes and hoping no one calls your name isn't leadership. Instead, grab your rifle and helmet, put "camouflage paint" on your face, and exclaim, "I'll do it, Sergeant!" It is no different in our world, less the rifle of course.

When you have a chance to put your neck on the line for a new sales campaign idea or battle an underwriting decision on behalf of one of your advisors, say "I'll do it!" as loud as you can and take the opportunity head-on. For the task to succeed it requires someone to take ownership and place themselves at some risk. Nothing is gained by taking the path of least resistance or hoping that things will just eventually get better at your branch. Become good at "hearing" opportunities in everyday circumstances to take control of situations and move them forward.

To achieve results this industry needs leadership, not just managers. For advisors it's a time in history that carries heavy responsibility as they deal with the challenge of the boomer demographic moving into a new stage of life and looking for financial advice. This situation calls for a leader with the "intestinal fortitude" to navigate their advisors through the noise, smoke, and confusion that lies ahead. The only way to get better at the craft of leadership is to get into the trenches and do the job.

Principle #5: Achieve Professional Competence

One of the elements of being believable as a leader is being credible. This is why for hundreds of years military organizations have promoted from within their ranks. You become a sergeant after first being a corporal and a private for several years. This allows individuals to gain experience and tests their skills in a kaleidoscope of challenging situations: at home and abroad, in peace and conflict.

The financial services industry is very similar: knowledgeable, competent people can be found within the advisor ranks. Managers who spend even a modest amount of time as an agent will have greater understanding and credibility than a manager parachuted in from "outside" the organization to lead the agency.

Time and experience are important but greatly complemented by education. Some of the most powerful ways to achieve professional competence in our industry is through earning designations such as Certified Financial Planner (CFP), Chartered Life Underwriter (CLU), and Elder Planning Counselor (EPC). Develop yourself by learning as much as possible about a wide variety of subjects, learn what is happening in our industry abroad as well as in your own country, and become a voracious reader of industry magazines and books. You will have a distinct advantage over another manager who hasn't sought out development of their craft since getting their life license many years ago.

It's hard expecting your advisors to strive to develop professionally if they don't see you doing it too. Share with your advisors the articles you've read, relevant resources you've found, and insights from courses that had an impact on you. By doing so your advisors will also strive to develop themselves professionally, benefiting the clients who prefer to work with advisors who continually sharpen and polish their skills.

Principle #6: Keep Your People Informed

Only by knowing what's happening in the entire theatre of operations can a soldier make the decisions required at a level where the work actually gets done. To remove a minefield at night requires you to know who is in front of you, who is behind you, and what is on either side of you. Technical skills are not enough to advance your agency. Being fantastic at insurance product design, sales processes, or wealth paperwork may help to a point but you have to be great with the people you interact with to show real value. I have seen many managers who are too comfortable in learning every detail of the job but not able to convey it or apply it to the people who need it most. Sometime agents just want to be told the answer quickly but a good manager takes the opportunity at hand to educate the "why" as well as the "what" or "how" of solving a problem.

The unknown is scary; it causes doubt that paralyses some and causes costly delays in decision-making in others. In the absence of accurate information, imagination takes over and the effectiveness of people wanes. Rumours cost time and effort to investigate and eradicate before your people are fully functional again. A distracted agent is a danger to themselves and others around them. Relative to our industry, give your advisors the "big picture" as a frame of context around the granular detail that pervades their day-to-day agenda. Keep them up to date on salient issues in the Canadian marketplace, government regulators, federal budgets, the financial industry, their company, the competition, product changes, and so on. It's important for them to do their jobs effectively and for them to provide this same "big picture" to the clients they service.

That Combat Leadership Course taught us that leadership is a privilege and not a right. This holds true whether you're in the military service or the financial service. So seek responsibility even if risky; reduce that risk by being professionally competent and providing the needed information to your people to do their job effectively. Now find a helmet and get in the trenches.

Principle #7: Ensure Your Direction is Understood, Supervised and Accomplished

Have you ever left a situation where you believe you have effectively communicated the task at hand only to discover the person has diligently completed it incorrectly? When assigning a project to a manager, instead of asking, "Do you understand?" ask "Did I explain that sufficiently?" The second phrasing allows someone to ask for additional information without feeling incompetent. Thereafter, provide appropriate supervision for the individual and difficulty of project at hand.

If you have some uncertainty with a new manager in terms of their skills, don't work over them, work beside them. This is a great way to supervise and teach all at the same time, and keep your own skills sharp.

As a combat engineer, I never sent troops over a bridge we built until I ensured the bridge was 100 percent complete, right down to the glow-sticks marking the entranceway. So too, you need to ensure the task has been accomplished before moving forward with other plans.

Principle #8: Appreciate Your Own Strengths and Weaknesses

Through innate abilities or skills developed, we discover what we are good at and what we are not good at in this business. Knowing your own strengths and weaknesses is important because it allows you to surround yourself with a team of people who are good at what you are not, and likely their weaknesses will be your strengths.

By developing "complementary" relationships with others, you can leverage their strengths and yours. This could be as simple as asking their feedback on an incentive program because you find you are not quite as creative as others, or perhaps having someone on your team who has a way with words proofread a potentially volatile email before you send it out to your advisors. Admitting weakness in a certain area and asking for support shows strength and creates a collaborative team.

Principle #9: Make Sound Plans and Timely Decisions

In the modern business environment, the speed and dynamics require us to control what we can and prepare for everything else. In World War II, General Patton once said, "A good plan on time is better than a great plan late." You've probably seen many an elaborate, detailed, and inspiring business plan created in January, but introduced to everyone in March and never looked at again. Without implementation, like a financial plan for a client, a plan is utterly worthless.

Leaders give directions to the group and they make decisions. That is what we get paid the "top half" of our incomes for: making the call when it needs to be made. We are never given enough time to make the perfect decision and often catastrophes will happen in the agency right in the middle of a campaign or when you're out of time. Weigh the pros and cons, trust your gut, and make the call. When it comes to my team, I have never reprimanded anyone for making a decision. I may educate them on other solutions they could have implemented after the fact but I do not want to douse the fire of people who think, take a chance of being wrong, and make a decision.

Principle #10: Lead by Example

This is the master principle and the king of the other nine. If you do not get this right, nothing else really matters. Once you accept a leadership position, you give up the right to have a bad day. Others in your office are watching you, judging the situation at hand, and basing their reactions largely on your behaviour and actions.

Genghis Khan is arguably one of history's most powerful military leaders. His troops followed him passionately; not because he created a power base steeped in fear but because he would share his followers' hardships and not ask them to do things he would not be willing to do himself. This behaviour inspired the men. For example, when his troops had no water, he stood up in front of them and emptied out his canteen as a powerful symbol of trust and a way to say he shared their suffering.

The intense fires that forge a good soldier are <u>Integrity</u> – refuse to deceive others or yourself, your behaviour must be congruent with your intentions, <u>Courage</u> – willingness to face hardship and do the job others would withdraw from, and <u>Loyalty</u> – in both directions of the chain of command, without supporting those above you and those who rely on your strength the system falls apart.

I have needed these elemental fires often in the face of extreme challenges in both my former career and my current. Remember the fires that forged you as a sales manager: your agents and your management team are counting on you to lead them in times of adversity. Give them a fire to rally around together with peers, to feel safe when sharing career concerns, and to provide a guiding light to what is possible in our profession.

How to Succeed in Personal Production and Management

Shawn Bellefeuille

You have three really great client appointments scheduled and it should lead to some good business, and then your phone rings. It's one of your high-priority clients asking to meet with you to go over details of their portfolio wondering if you can make some improvements. At the same time, you get a text from an advisor you coach asking for some of your time today to talk about some urgent client matters. Sound familiar? I bet it does.

Being a financial advisor is demanding. Being a manager is also demanding. And you're doing both? One might say it's impossible though I'm here to tell you it IS possible but be ready for the challenge and ever changing conditions of every single day. I have put together key information that has helped guide me through these types of situations as well as other scenarios you might encounter.

First things first, you need to make a commitment to your agents and make it clear to those you mentor that they are a priority. Don't forget, when you hired them you most likely promised to be there for them and help them succeed. We have chosen a career to serve, meaning that if they are in a jam they can count on your help even though you already have a busy day. This is not that hard to do, it takes a commitment on your part. It is also an important teaching moment for your advisors to see how you can manage and control your own schedule.

Schedule everything!

You need to have total control of your schedule at all times. I suggest that you color code your client appointments and prospecting tasks and you can also color code your coaching and fieldwork time. Encourage your team to come see you during that time because it's dedicated to them. This arrangement removes any discomfort they may have to come to you for advice but more importantly, it will remove the incessant visits you get during the day prompted by "I just have a quick question." This is a must-do practise and also the best way to teach your new advisors how to manage their own practise. Remember to practise what you preach. These business tools will help them succeed as much as you.

Goals!

Share your personal production goals with your team. Some might think that this could be demotivating or perhaps even seen as boastful. Not at all! You need them to know that their manager also does the same work they do and that you set goals in just the same way you require of them. Most of all it will help push you to become more successful because your goals are public and therefore it makes you very accountable. Nothing makes you seem more relevant to them than seeing you in the field selling on a consistent basis, qualifying for company campaigns, and attending prestigious the Million Dollar Roundtable (MDRT). Your success will encourage their success.

Joint Fieldwork

This is where our most important work is done. You need to make sure to demonstrate how to conduct appointments and to evaluate what you expect from your agents. Yes, that's right, I suggest show versus tell. I am not suggesting that you stop in class training, self-study modules, or role playing as these are important aspects of training but no amount of this can replace face-to-face training time. The more time you invest in joint fieldwork at the beginning, the quicker they are likely to taste success. It will also free up valuable time down the road for you to work with a new candidate.

New advisors must become Interdependent

A great teaching moment is to bring your new advisors on your appointments. Show them that an appointment is an appointment, not a social call. Establish that when you follow a process everything works out. Remember your new advisors or even experienced ones are always watching you. I found that an influential training tool was to include them on the compensation of a sale that I'd made while they joined me. Don't just give it away; have them do proper follow ups with the underwriting department and other administrative tasks that are necessary. This goes a long way toward minimizing your workload while showing them how you work in a practical way.

Select people you can work with

I cannot stress this enough. Do not cut this corner because it could make your life miserable by increasing your workload, making you less productive and causing stress while doing managerial duties. This is an industry that has a 15 percent retention rate after four years as shown in LIMRA's 2010 report. If you do not focus on your selection process then you will become a part of this statistic. Make sure you have an ideal candidate profile and you stick to what works while making tweaks and changes wherever needed.

That being said, you must also take ownership of any bad recruit and fire fast! Only hire people you can work with. However, if you think they might be better suited for another manager to coach them, this may be a good time-managing opportunity for you.

Finally, have strength in numbers! Know your numbers; you don't have time to waste. Make sure you know what you are working towards, whether that is qualifying for a company sales conference or MDRT. Track it, know it, and breathe it. I use a planner to track client calls, recruiting calls, and many daily tasks to help keep me to my goals. Again, what a great lesson for your junior advisors: demonstrating what a winning advisor needs to do!

You have chosen a boundless path in financial services. Not only are you helping your clients, you are also giving back to an industry that I'm sure has been good to you. This might be one of the reasons you chose to build and lead a team of advisors. Financial services will go through challenges in the future. We need to be dynamic and evolving in this industry in the years to come and I am confident that good advisors being led by exceptional leaders will give our industry the ability to survive the changes and adaptations of our continuously evolving society. We need to bring new people into our industry and give them the tools to help people while building a great career.

When you experience a tough day, you will be prepared for it; you will embrace it and be ready to tackle the challenges ahead.

By Shawn Bellefeuille, CFP, CLU, CHS
Desjardins Financial Security Independent Network
Ottawa Financial Centre, Associate Manager
GAMA International Canada President - 2015 to present

Building an Exemplary Leadership Brand

Izumi Miki McGruer

Having the privilege of coming into this industry over 25 years ago, I've watched time inevitably march on. Although our perspective grows through the changes and challenges, the fundamentals of good business and leadership from my perspective have never altered. Therein lies the often heartbreaking conundrum I believe many new managers face as they valiantly struggle to juggle the critical glass balls associated with our management responsibilities.

In these seemingly complex times it is absolutely paramount that new managers understand the difference between establishing a strong "management brand" and building an exemplary "leadership brand." The latter is associated with consistently achieving excellence in all aspects of our tremendous career while the former does not necessarily put one in a position to lead or influence to any meaningful end despite the expected achievement of results.

Antoine de Saint-Exupery's Little Prince observed:

"And now here is my secret, a very simple secret: It is only with the heart that one can see rightly; what is essential is invisible to the eye."

Throughout my life, I have been blessed with having many wonderful mentors whose "leadership brand" was awe-inspiring. Despite their individual uniqueness, my heroes all believed passionately in three things:

1. Being of service to others is a privilege
2. Every individual is unique and talented
3. Positive attitude is everything

For these individuals the art of "being present" in order to manifest their passionate beliefs was at the core of their greatness. The physical aspect of "being present" is literally the paradox of prioritizing poise and stillness into one's movements. When this visual intensity of purpose is combined with a tranquility of mind, the sharer knows that you are 100 percent their dominant focus. The subsequent message of care and respect non-verbally communicated is far more powerful than words could ever be. I continue to marvel at how developing the ability to listen objectively with a calm head and heart remains tantamount to helping others take action that is meaningful to them.

Over my time as manager, I have observed this invaluable skill mastered to be a game-changing catalyst for exponentially increasing one's leadership influence and real value to others. It is the ultimate leadership example that creates convergence across all organizational synergies. I once read that the three most powerful phrases in all human relations were:

1. Maybe you are right
2. Your heart knows
3. I'll be there

Simply put, taking the time and having the grace to genuinely care and listen to those around us is foundational to building a culture of excellence. It grants us permission to remove barriers to success because we understand from another's perspective what is truly important and relevant to them.

In today's world building a strong "leadership brand" requires an unflinching commitment to our values compass. The metrics-driven maps of our organizations help us to understand where we need to go but our internal values-driven compass determines how we will get there successfully together. Our leadership-values compass is what encourages us to grow professionally, motivates us to prioritize the attainment of our professional designations, inspires us to demonstrate responsible stewardship in our community, and helps us earn the right to lead by example. These success behaviours quickly become the difference between being able to provide insight versus information, and inspired innovation versus legacy solutions.

Once you have defined your "leadership-values compass," the development of a "Values Covenant" becomes second nature and allows you to crystallize and communicate what you believe. Your Values Covenant is a robust document that ensures clarity of culture, communication, and purpose. Although a traditional Mission, Vision, and Values Statement remains fundamental to a well-crafted business plan, the "Values Covenant" differentiates itself from this traditional document in that it represents the practical synthesis of your "leadership-values compass" and speaks to how we live together.

A "Values Covenant" clearly outlines our leadership expectations of one another, gives everyone an understanding of how we are expected to treat each other, and clearly defines what we celebrate as success. When thoughtfully constructed, a "Values Covenant" can easily metamorphose into a practical "Success Matrix" triage tool. This multi-faceted four-quadrant grid defines success from a quantitative and qualitative perspective. It also facilitates the segmentation of advisors into "doing it" or "not doing it" and "doing it our way" or "not our way" categories as it relates to the requisite leadership qualities, processes, and performance metrics that lie at the heart of your success culture.

Doing it Not our way	Doing it Our way ☺
Not doing it Not our way	Not doing it Our way

In the advisor selection process, I have also found the "Success Matrix" to be a valuable tool as its psychographic elements serve as a practical benchmark for behavioural interview examples. This matrix creates transparency for tactical performance management and skill development; it elegantly identifies future leaders through its weighted focus on desired leadership qualities and organically creates mentoring opportunities as champions of process, training, and character naturally percolate through. The "Success Matrix" ultimately develops a culture of success anchored in substance, which increases candidate referrals as you have helped to create a great place to build a business.

A wise man once told me that achieving excellence as a manager was all about creating magnificent gardens. He explained to me that my long-term success was dependent on finding the most precious of seeds, planting them with care, fiercely protecting them from the elements, and showering them with water, fertilizer, and sunshine so that their full potential would come to fruition. I have always understood that the grand design for our gardens lies tangibly in the maps we all carry but nurturing a garden that is bursting with splendiferous beauty and unimagined surprises requires something infinitely more profound: an unwavering discipline, patience, head, heart, and a steady compass hand.

By Izumi Miki McGruer, CFP, CLU, ChFC, CHS
Director, Regional Development Manager
Freedom 55 Financial

Managing People is Exhausting – So Get Help!

Warren Miles-Pickup

Managing people is exhausting. Managing A-type people is beyond exhausting. Managing A-type entrepreneurs is equivalent to running a marathon twice a day, every day. So how does a successful field manager survive? By building a team that can turn marathons into a relay race.

The most successful managers in the financial advisory business have built incredibly strong teams of support staff to help drive their efforts. This support staff can include other managers, administrative professionals, technology trainers, and assistants. A source of support that is commonly overlooked though is that of the external partner or product manufacturer—the supplier.

These individuals can be utilized to provide training and resources that aren't necessarily available to most managers and support staff. Allowing these partners to assume a part of the relay race can take a lot of pressure off you as well as your support staff. The best part is you don't have to pay them, and in many cases, they may even provide financial resources to your office.

A good external partner will likely provide you with some or all of the following resources:

» Sponsorship for branch events
» Sales and product training
» Industry training and updates
» Promotional materials for giveaways and charity events

A great partner will take this a step further and it involves sharing your business goals with them and having them tailor conversations with your staff to assist you in exceeding those goals. The partners will ensure that your agency's goals are tied directly to theirs and may even sacrifice their goals in the short term to deepen their relationship with you and your team for greater success in the long term.

The strength of the relationship you have with this person can result in better service for your staff, faster resolution of issues, innovative sales strategies, shared industry knowledge, and greater investment in your business. All of this will result in a significantly stronger team and the removal of large amounts of stress and effort for you, allowing you to focus on the other tasks that require your attention.

The question is how do you get someone who you don't directly employ to take an active and integrated role in your business? The external partners you work with have their own goals and targets that they are required to accomplish too. Recognizing this and understanding your partner's goals is the best way to align both sets of interests. Not many field managers take the time to sit with their external partners and understand those goals, this can be an advantage for you to leverage. The great managers take this opportunity to the next level by committing to accomplishing a defined portion of that goal. So where do you start?

Build Rapport

Take the time to develop a relationship with your supplier. Each time they visit your agency you can ask they take five minutes to have a conversation with you at the end of their time at your office. Whether the conversation is small talk and personal or focuses directly onto business at hand, taking a few minutes to build rapport will ingratiate this person to you and create a desire for them to support you.

Most suppliers spend the majority of their time listening to clients and agents; take a few moments to ask about them and their lives. Everyone loves to talk about themselves. Learning about their life and their family will build a layer of trust into your relationship that will have significant benefits. The more comfortable they are with you, the more information they may share with you about your staff and issues occurring in your agency you may not be aware of. This could allow you the opportunity to stop problems before they even start.

Be Creative

Certainly it is in a supplier's best interest to develop ways to interact with you and your team. Top managers will take the lead; how you work with your supplier often requires that you come up with ways to involve them in your business. The more creative and dynamic these interactions are the more likely the supplier will want to support your business goals.

Here are some ideas:

» Speaking opportunities with your agents (meetings, luncheons, training sessions)
» Invitation to events (gala and recognition events, AGM's, client seminars and branch socials)
» Allowing sponsorship for agency events and campaign kick-offs
» Developing business plans together with the supplier
» Formally introducing the supplier to new agents as they are contracted
» Promoting supplier to staff members, management teams, other agencies and companies
» Direct purchase of products to incent agents for higher production levels

More successful events will involve combining a number of the examples above. Inviting a supplier to join your staff on rewards trips for your agents where the supplier can sponsors and present at a fun event on the trip is a great place to start. This type of activity makes the supplier feel part of the team and allows them to build relationships with your agency beyond a strictly business-oriented one. This benefits the supplier beyond just the immediate sale and helps them to develop long-term relationships. The better the relationships they have with your staff the more likely they are to use their resources to support your business.

Recognize Ambition

Many suppliers are sales people that have ambitions within their own organization to climb up the corporate ladder. If the supplier is one of these people then helping to support their career ambitions can lead you to becoming their top client—and top clients get supported the most. When given the opportunity reach out to the supplier's supervising manager to offer positive feedback or constructive advice. This also allows you to have a positive conversation with the upper management at your supplier's firm, which again will result in you receiving better support and service going forward on a company-to-company basis. Managers that even make small gestures like this are likely to receive a very positive response from their supplier.

Become their Most Important Client

This may seem intuitive but it is rarely practised. Being someone's most important client does not necessarily mean that you purchase the majority of their products. It could mean that you provide them with the greatest level of support or make their job easy when they are coming to your office. By promoting them to your staff and allowing them unfettered access, they will feel more welcome and involved in your agency. Making them feel like they are part of your team creates an emotional connection to your staff that will lead to a significantly greater level of support and partnership.

Take advantage of the benefits of working with your supplier, but make sure you're attracting and partnering with the great ones. In the end, both of you will be better off for the extra effort.

By Warren Miles-Pickup, BA
Wealth Sales Director, Sun Life Financial

Points to Remember from this Section

1. Remember our industry is an Essential Service
2. Move everyday thinking from weekly/monthly to quarterly/annually
3. Build a Management Bench quickly

Now add points you want to remember or refer back to:

-
-
-
-
-
-
-

Notes:

_____

_____

_____

_____

_____

_____

Section 2

Finding People for Your Agency

Recruiting as a Way of Life

There are not enough of us already, and we are surrounded by people who need the financial advice we provide.

At the end of the day, it all comes down to bringing new people into your organization. You can be a master administrator, compliance officer, sales trainer, business visionary, and understand financial products inside and out but if you cannot attract new talent to your agency, none of the rest really matters. Like a long train that's lost the locomotive engine, the inertia you have built thus far will carry you along for a while but will eventually stop moving completely. And, I'm sorry to say, that's when your agency dies. You are either growing or decaying your business. You simply can't make your way to greatness by keeping your growth engine in neutral!

Often a manager's career lives or dies with their ability to recruit. There is a saying often heard, "I can recruit myself out of any problem" and it is absolutely true. Maybe you have a group of senior advisors with bad attitudes, under-performing five-year advisors, or have inherited a culture of apathy or poison. It can all be changed with new recruits who you have found, selected, and trained yourself. In this industry, if you are a great recruiter watch how many doors open for you!

Personally, I was not a "rock star" recruiter, my wife Julie certainly was, but I was good and consistently so. I went from advisor to running my own branch in under five years. In another five years, I led our agency to being a top quality branch in Canada. This was a culmination of bringing on aspiring new agents while keeping ones that were already performing well. For every struggling agent to whom we said goodbye we hired two new agents. This formula works; -1 failing agent + 2 recruits = +1 agency growth.

In a very real way, sales managers are the "sales force" of the financial industry in North America. If we aren't recruiting new recruits, certainly no one else will do it for us. A person has to be introduced to this career, often several times over many years before we catch the right person at the right time to be successful in this role. People will not join this industry on their own accord for two common reasons: they don't know about it or what they know isn't correct. People out there simply do not wake up one morning and say, "I want to buy life insurance today," so neither do they say, "I want to sell life insurance today." It just does not happen naturally; there is more likelihood of a unicorn walking through your office foyer than your next top agent.

I have yet to hear about any large insurance broker or career agency model that has an efficient, dedicated, and local department doing this critical task for them successfully. Except in rare circumstances, no one other than sales managers is suggesting this career opportunity to anyone. High school and university career counsellors aren't doing it, employment agencies aren't doing it, outplacement consultants aren't doing it, and friends and family probably aren't suggesting it to those they know who sorely need a career change.

Every year people leave, retire, or are let go from the industry. On a good year, you will lose 15 percent of your advisors. If you don't recruit, it won't be long before you won't be in the industry either. At the very least, you need to replace the people who are leaving to be neutral. If you want to grow your agency by 5 percent, for example in a 40-agent office, you'd have to grow by 2 people. In order to grow by 5 percent, plus replace the 15 percent you will likely lose naturally, you have to recruit 8 people in that year to minimally develop your agency.

If on average a sales manager recruits three agents per year, this equals over forty-five people in a fifteen-year career. One manager can affect tens of thousands of clients in the community by obtaining the financial products and advice through these recruits during their careers. From a production point of view, each one of the agents can place tens of millions of dollars for insurance coverage and control tens of millions of dollars of investments for these clients. As you can see, the impact even an averagely performing sales manager has is absolutely staggering!

A common mistake I see with new managers is the attitude that they will recruit one agent per year who is a "super star" and therefore don't need to recruit any more that year. This outlook is disastrous for both the manager and the agency. The numbers always show that if three recruits come into the organization then one will be a steady survivor, one will quit within a couple of years, and one could be a rock star. Despite everything we may try and the experience we have collected, it's still a gamble as to which candidate will be a rock star out of the three and which one will be gone next year.

Too often I've heard a new manager say they only want to "hire top quality" and they can naturally "spot talent." If you can actually do that repeatedly for your career then congratulations, you have found a magic bullet no one else has discovered in the history of the industry. However, for the rest of us, I've found to be successful in recruiting it is simply a numbers game, especially during the prospecting phase. Talk to everyone and anyone, keep your recruiting antennae up at all times, and good things will happen. I promise.

Who make the best agents?

The common denominator of the best recruits is that they want something more from their work and their life than they have today. They may be passed over for promotion, they can be downsized suddenly, they are not recognized or appreciated, they're tired of working for someone else, or they are new to the country and need a white-collar career. At the end of the day, I've found the best candidates want control of their income, vacations, work schedule, job security, and such. They don't want to wait at the end of the year to be told by their supervisor they have done a good job and earned a whopping 1 percent salary increase. Or worse, that they've done a good job but the company is not in the position to even grant an increase!

You want to look for attributes, the DNA if you will, of the person not the career choice they are currently in. I've had agents in my team over the years come from a wide range of occupations including diesel mechanics, nurses, engineers, and even pastors. If I had simply read their resume looking for a financial or entrepreneurial background, I would have missed a huge opportunity, for them and us. On the other hand, some of the lowest performing agents I've dealt with have sometimes come with their life licenses in hand, belonged to MENSA, and had run their own companies before meeting us. It is not what they have done but what they're capable of that I'm interested in.

Some attributes that I have seen as clues to a great agent are:

- » Impressive character
- » Strong people skills: easy to talk to, picks up conversation easily
- » Demonstrable integrity in difficult situations
- » Passion to help others
- » Overcome something significant like a divorce or death of a loved one
- » Dignity and positive outlook of self and others
- » Belief for the future, mindful of coming changes
- » Drive for a better income and lifestyle
- » Desire for meaningful work
- » Tenacity and perseverance in the face of adversity, like competitive sports

If you find a candidate with all these attributes, thank the financial services gods, but it is rare. More likely you will find someone with some of these attributes. I find it easier to trim a flame that's burning bright to be something useful than trying to get a fire started with wet wood. You have to have something to work with in a candidate; trust the selection and training process to bring out their best chances of being a great agent.

One attribute that is hard to quantify but I think it's a big predictor of success; you'll know it when you hear it—personal scars obtained in life. By this I don't mean to inspect their bodies for physical marks or deformities, but look for evidence of a pain that they had to survive, something that has forged their metal a little bit stronger than other people walking around out there—a person who has come through a hard divorce from a spouse, who said they wouldn't amount to anything, or an immigrant who achieved a MBA in their former country but is now stacking boxes in a warehouse, or someone who has lost someone close to cancer and now has a "story" to tell others. These people have a hot fire pushing them and it has seen them through the kind of tough times that can make other people curl up into a fetal position. Find these candidates: they need you and you need them.

Candidate Welcome Letter - Example

You have found your perfect candidate, now what? In our insanely busy lives, I find having a fast, easy-to-follow system makes things simpler for everyone. I have made several of these quick next-step pieces and they can be prepared beforehand and administered by your staff as needed.

The letter template below is a piece that I immediately send to a candidate once they have successfully completed an online aptitude test such as a Career Profile, DISC, or SalesPro. You can simply customize the letter below or use it as inspiration to create your own welcome letter that fits your agency's needs and culture. Ensure to mail it to their home as people still notice when they receive mail versus email these day. Remember you want their spouse to see it too!

Dear (Candidate name),

Firstly, congratulations on enrolling in the licensing program to obtain your insurance qualification as well as passing the aptitude questionnaire with flying colours. I believe you will impress yourself on how well you do as we journey through the steps together.. As you complete the selection process I know you are eager to start working with people and learning how to be a financial advisor with our team. Secondly, I hope you take some time to read this letter as it's about you.

Sooner or later people wonder whether their career is actually an extension of themselves and what it says about them. Socrates said, "A life unexamined is not worth living" and I believe moments of self-analysis and career-analysis are opportunities to examine if it's time for a change. You have shown courage to begin that examination and are open to opportunities others would not see. Socrates would be proud!

Significance is achieved through helping others, not money or trophies. It's about the impact you have on others by delivering intrinsic value measured by the size of the problems you solve for others. Our industry solves serious problems for North Americans in the 21st century.

- We protect people who depend on others so they have peace of mind when that person is no longer able to care of them
- We provide worry-free retirement with an income people can't outlive so they can keep their independence and enjoy retirement
- We protect people's assets when they get sick or unable to work so they can focus on getting better and retain their financial plans
- We provide legacy for families and businesses so that what they have built carries on

We talk to people about what is important, not just about what's popular.

I am looking for a person wanting to do something extraordinary and impactful with 2016. My entire resource team, along with the designated mentor I have arranged, will work with both of us to ensure you have a head start to a great career.

I personally owe this company everything. It has given me an incredible lifestyle; it challenges and develops me, allowed me to have balance, and has given me a chance to re-invent myself from a soldier to a white-collar professional that helps others for a living. My only regret is that I didn't start this career sooner in life.

Living this life should not happen by chance; instead, it should happen by choice. Make your time stand for something special. I look forward to meeting you again.

Be great!

(your name and signature)

Where to Find Good Recruits

As the saying goes, "It's always in the last place you look." If you are still looking then you haven't found it yet, right? So keep looking!

The best recruits today are clerks setting out the vegetables at your local grocery store, a long-haul truck driver, a dentist with carpal tunnel syndrome, a fitness instructor, a soldier, a diesel mechanic, and the cancer survivor. The point being, they are not looking or acting like agents currently, have no financial background nor already working at commission sales.

So you need to look everywhere, constantly. As you could see from the previous chapter, recruits can come from any industry, any path of life, so keep recruiting methods constant and expansive. Your mantra needs to be: Does everyone in my community know I'm recruiting? Until you can answer that question affirmatively, you have work to do. Since you will never be able to answer that question affirmatively, recruiting is constant in our role. You can never say "I'm good enough now for recruit candidates."

Referrals from Your Advisors

A good place to start, if you're fortunate enough, is with existing advisors within your hallways. They know what the career is about and what it takes to succeed, they know your agency culture intimately and your leadership style. Moreover, your agents likely have a large network of people they associate with on a favourable basis. Typically, advisor referrals come with time and trust as a result of you helping them out with career development, battling a big case with underwriting departments, or assisting with difficult situations or clients. Subsequently, often advisor referrals come to the senior managers in the organization (assuming that senior manager has been respectful of existing advisors) because they have had more time interacting with agents.

Don't think your advisors always give you names or business cards solely because of altruism. The "what's in it for me" factor is often at play for anyone you're dealing with in business. Perhaps they are looking for a successor or a prodigy because their own adult child hasn't shown interest in joining the business with them. Maybe they are looking for a business partner in the future or even a backup plan if the current partnership doesn't pan out. While they might be slightly interested in having the referred person in the agency, they certainly don't want to deal with the headache of interviewing and selection, background checks, licensing, sales and product training, joint fieldwork, and so on. That they leave for you, and that's your role. Everybody wins if the referred candidate is successful in joining the team.

Whether it's part of a plan or naturally happens, I've found many senior advisors like to pick partners and successors from the junior advisors already in their organization. From a bit of a distance they can observe the rookie's behaviour, work ethic, integrity, and, of course, success before approaching the rookie with a serious proposition.

I have found the success ratio to be between 5:1 and 7:1 for an advisor referral to bring on a new advisor. Hands down, it is the best and quickest source for getting a recruit on board in your agency. In my experience, it compares against 200:1 for advertising, 100:1 for career fairs and bulk mail-outs, 80:1 for university graduates, 50:1 for e-resumes database mining, 20:1 for personal observation, and 15:1 for well-trained centres of influence.

You can make it part of your agency's recognition program but don't just think money motivates agents to refer to you. Make it a big deal in front of their peers at agency meetings and AGMs when someone joins your team through this method. Even have your regional VP join you all for a celebratory lunch or present a plaque to show your appreciation.

Centres of Influence (COI's)

After advisor referrals, you can look here for good candidates. However, like agent referrals it can take time to see results. You need to train a Centre of Influence (COI) and this can take months or even years to get good quality candidates consistently from them. This recruiting source also tends to be available to mature managers in the business but if you are a new manager, you can begin building your Centres of Influence now.

Start by building a COI by identifying people you know are well connected to large communities of people. A good example that has worked for me in the past is retired advisors (especially those who referred good people to you when they were active with your agency), local politicians, Chamber of Commerce leaders, senior members of local Boards of Trade, heads of Rotary Clubs, and even competing financial organizations have been good sources over the years.

When you meet with your COIs explain exactly what you are looking for. Be crystal clear on specific candidate characteristics or high-potential markets versus general statements of "I'm looking for good salespeople this year." If the description is too general it can get lost in the white noise of life and will not be recollected when a good prospect walks in front of them. Saying instead, "I am looking for someone who stands out and a) who lives in this geographic area; b) has an additional language skill; c) is within this age demographic; and d) has entrepreneurial DNA." It's like game hunting and simply saying to your partner, "tell me when you see anything" can lead to some interesting hunting results brought home to cook but likely your day won't be successful.

A tricky situation can arise from well-meaning COIs: they try to qualify good candidates before telling you or introducing you to them at an initial meeting. Perhaps they want to impress you with their super candidate or fear wasting your time with people who will be washed out of the selection process or even want to ensure the candidate knows a lot about the career before investigating further with you. This is a problem for a couple of reasons.

First, you may not know this 'pre-screen' is happening for a long time. For example, over lunch one day you ask why they haven't introduced any candidate to you lately and they respond that they have talked to lots of people about the role, talked about commission and selling life insurance but unfortunately no one is interested right now! After you pick your head off the restaurant table and find yourself grinding your teeth you will come to realize this isn't the COI's fault; it's yours. They likely thought they were helping you the entire time.

Part of grooming a good COI is teaching them where their part of the process ends and yours begins. They need to trust you with whomever they send your way: if they don't or can't, then solve the problem or don't proceed with the arrangement. Even if you can now salvage your COI and put them on the right track, unfortunately, there may have been several good candidates lost to the wind already. A hard lesson learned indeed and a missed chance for you and the candidates.

Secondly, even with exposure to your industry and hours spent with you learning about who makes a good advisor and the opportunities at your location, there is no way they know enough to select someone for your agency and in fact, they are not allowed to! What they may know, assuming they get even half the pertinent details correct, isn't sufficient to deal with the inevitable objections and concerns the candidate will naturally have. We are asking people to potentially leave their jobs and consider a career change to a commissioned role selling client-resistant and intangible products. If they are that good at it and truly find success in this arena then hire them as a recruiting manager on your team!

Talk to your COIs every two weeks by phone but face to face is obviously preferable. Only use email and text messages for spontaneous contact and "thinking of you" moments. Have no more than a handful of COIs at a time or you will not have the time or energy to connect with them frequently enough to be at the front of their minds. I personally like keeping about five COIs going at one time. I set up pop-up calendar reminders weekly to think of a reason to reach out to them, preferably about a reciprocal referral situation I have for them or an update on how their last referred recruit has been doing at our branch.

Make sure you take COI's out for breakfasts on their birthday and business anniversaries throughout the year. If they do refer a recruit who joins your agency, I would say a nice dinner out with the COI is in order. Perhaps even invite the rookie's spouse too. Make the moment special and when you do refer to that moment, it will bring back positive memories for all.

Social Media/Electronic Communities

Historically, websites like Workopolis were effective when they were first available but now these hunting fields are saturated with sales organizations contacting people and filled with resumes of people who are actually quite happy in their current job but are just "kicking tires" or seeing if they are still desirable in the job markets. This medium has lost most of its recruiting impact. In place of resume databases, look to LinkedIn to identify people and ask them for introductions to those they are connected to, and then get in front of them. Remember you will not sell people on the idea of a career change over the phone and that you are asking only for an opportunity to get to know them better and discover what interests them. Once you meet face to face over a coffee you can start to talk about the details of the career and look for interest.

Situational Prospecting (aka Personal Observation)

This is a long-standing recruiting method, and one of my favourite ways to recruit. For example, you are having a relaxing business lunch with a colleague or perhaps attending a friend's wedding. You realize your server is really attentive and detail-oriented. You wonder if they might be under-valued in their current role and you switch into recruiting mode. You give them your card or obtain their card and indicate that you are looking for a few good people this year and suggest you get together at your office for an off-the-record chat. Do not turn this casual connection into a dramatic, agenda-driven recruiting trial or else you might scare them off from meeting with you later.

Sometimes it feels more complimentary to the individual of interest to receive a call from someone else in your office. In the scenario above, where you see an interesting prospect, instead of calling them yourself, you pass the contact information to another manager in the office. They call the lead and say, "You assisted a colleague of mine yesterday, she was impressed and gave me your business card. She said you had talent in problem solving and were thinking of moving to our area. I would enjoy an opportunity to meet to learn more about what talents you have and where you see yourself in the next couple of years."

Career Fairs and Employment Trade Shows

It might come as a surprise that career fairs are not as effective a recruiting tool as the event planners who organize them would have you believe, at least for our industry anyway. At career fairs, attending individuals tend to be handing their resumes out to everyone and may just be interested in seeing what's out there without a goal of actually getting a job. Moreover, that is what the actual job seekers are looking for: a job. They are largely not people who are looking to be self-employed! You might get lots of good activity of people completing questionnaires and you will give out goodies and boxes of business cards but most will not make it as far as meeting you for a coffee. Like cold-calling as a last resort for struggling agents, a sales manager's reliance on career fairs may be avoiding other "active" recruiting opportunities. It feels busy to a new manager, but there are better places to prospect.

Career Presentations

Once a quarter or twice a year you can organize an event where you have the full attention of qualified potential candidates to favourably present the opportunity you have and then motivate people in the audience to move a step closer. First, find the audience or else it will be a pretty lonely event! Typically, you use people already in your agency's recruiting pipeline and it's a good venue to orientate new centres of influence.

Ask anyone who has shown an interest in a career change to attend, put posters up in employment centres, or even ask those candidates who have been in your prospecting funnel for a while and need another nudge to move up the selection process or out. Formally invite them (mail a letter to their home address) to an evening of wine and appetizers amongst other people who are also looking at a career move. The setting can be as big or small as you want it to be. If you can, arrange the date to coincide with your VP's visit to your branch or include another impressive speaker.

Tell those you're inviting to bring someone whose opinion they trust to join them. This may be their spouse (someone whose life could be significantly affected by their decision to move to a new career), a friend, or a mentor. This outreach can serve two functions. Firstly, it increases the number of attendees, which makes a positive impression on the other guests and drives energy into your event and therefore your presentation. Secondly, these additional people, who obviously your candidate trusts, will give them their feedback anyway so better to have the information delivered firsthand by you than rely on the retention, comprehension, and translation of pertinent information of the candidate. Too many times I have had an enthusiastic candidate be even more motivated to join our organization after these events to only be submarined by a confused or skeptical spouse or friend when they get home.

I have successfully run these sessions from our local boardrooms to memorable offsite venues such as helicopter hangers to fire halls to renting movie theatres. The events should start on time, run no longer than 45 minutes, and allow some time for questions and networking. Ensure that the manager or COI who invited the candidate attends to not only initially connect with each person but more importantly to connect with them at the end where enthusiasm is high and the next follow-up meeting can be arranged.

At this event you want to show a) why join the financial industry, b) why join our particular company and, c) why your branch is the best place to start their new career. Attendees can be in a group setting where they can be a bit anonymous, learn from other people's questions, and even confirm their understanding before making a decision (one way or another) about the career. Have handouts for them to take something tangible home with them but don't burden them with too much stuff. I prefer to keep the amount of marketing materials to a minimum at first but always make sure to include objective third-party articles on what to consider when making a career move to our industry.

The more senior managers in your office will often give their opinions (whether asked or not) on your recruiting ideas but take their advice with a grain of salt. Just because they got the results they did when they tried it before does not mean you will get the same results when you do. You are a different person with different skills trying it at a different time and venue with likely a different angle of approach. Keep trying new things, you will find your niche.

Once a pool of candidates has been established, time should be spent thinking about the candidates that are the best fit for what the manager is looking for and invite those candidates to go through a multi-step selection process. This process can vary between organizations, but no matter what model, virtually all candidates need to go through interviewing, obtaining a license and background checks.

In my experience, organizations that select too fast are looking for part-time agents or for a large number of selling agents as fast as possible by dropping the selection time and criteria and lowering the quality of the advisors. In contrast, those organizations that have a multi-faceted selection process with higher requirements are looking for full-time professional advisors and the organization wants to make sure it is not a mistake for the candidate or the business to get them in too fast. It is nobody's interest, for any industry, to move so fast that a mistake is made and somebody is put in the career they are not suited for.

A great analogy is a water faucet; if you have little or no filters, the quality of the water is going to be apparent, and bad. The more filters you put into the water source the cleaner the water you're getting out of it and the better the taste. However, if you put too many filters on that process you will get too little water coming out of the faucet. The trick is to find the balance of having good selection criteria and to respectfully apply that criterion to your organization but not to arbitrarily raise the bar to burdensome requirements. You will lose good candidates by doing this. You want to make sure you have good quality agents and be able to move them into a career in a reasonable amount of time. The trick in all this is to find the balance.

From this pool, 25 percent of a junior manager's time should be spend in working with their identified candidates to move forward into the selection process. This will be done in the form of interviews, needed paper work, tutoring through the licensing studies, and so on. Ideally, a manager should spend 1-2 hours either face to face or on the phone with every candidate they have in their recruiting funnel. During the latter stages of the selection process, most of the time will be spent with the candidate and not the manager. The manager is simply keeping the candidate accountable and providing resources and encouragement throughout the process. In the prospecting stage, most of the effort is spent by the manager and not the candidate.

It has been said many times by our industry that the motto for the new manager should be "recruit or die." So if you find yourself alone in the woods and survival is at stake, you would spend a significant amount of your time looking for shelter, food, and water. All other activities to that are secondary. The same is true with prospecting for new agents, be complacent at your own peril.

'Hunting' for an Advisor - Checklist

- What do you offer the successful candidate that is interested? List five impactful points you will memorize and be ready to use when hunting.
  - ○
  - ○
  - ○
  - ○
  - ○
- Define target geographic area (where will you be hunting)
- List of current advisors and where they live in your region (identify gaps in agency coverage)
- Define target advisor roles (what you are hunting for to bring back)
  - Advisor
  - Living Benefits Specialists (disability, LTC, etc.)
  - Manager
  - Licensed Associates
  - Administrative Assistant or Staff
- Define characteristics of the target person (who are you hunting)
  - Age
  - Languages
  - Marital status
  - Income range
  - Reputation in town
  - Current career frustrations
- Define goal and timeline for the role you need to fill in your agency
- Identify opportunities within agency for:
  - Succession Planning
  - New neighbourhood
  - Mentoring program available
  - Known advisor retirement in the next year
  - Block of business to be released (or give a 'starter block' to right rookie)
  - Targeted skillset or language

- Map of the area of the geographic area you want a candidate to work within
- Vital statistics of the area, review most recent census for:
  - average income
  - total population and growth rate
  - labour force by industries
  - unemployment rate
  - age and occupation bands
  - business formation and failures
  - family size
  - education level
  - male/female ratio
  - non-working population
  - housing types (detached homes, condo, townhouse, etc.)
  - immigration and languages spoken
- Identify competition within industry in your area of responsibility
- Complimentary businesses in your community to educate what you're hunting for
  - Legal offices
  - Employment services
  - Accountant and book-keeping services
  - Real estate agencies
  - Business to Business Associations
  - Mortgage specialists
  - Health professionals and Long term care facilities
  - General insurance and Automobile
  - Notary public
  - Funeral homes
  - Banks and credit unions
  - Investment institutions
  - New immigrant associations and services
  - Fee-for-service nurse care

- o Medical Equipment stores
- o Day care facilities
- Post-secondary institutions
  - o Colleges offering BBA, CFP and CLU designations
  - o Universities and vocational schools
  - o Technical institutions
- Business to visit that have commission salespeople:
  - o Furniture and mattress stores
  - o Audio/Video stores
  - o Car dealerships
  - o General insurance outlets
  - o Hospitality (hotels and restaurants)
  - o Cell phone outlets
  - o Retail department stores that have bonuses
  - o Office and computer equipment
  - o Travel agencies

"A High 5 for Recruiting" - Exercise

This is a great method for honing your recruiting craft between interviews, when stuck in traffic, or preparing for a challenging first interview. While other managers are staring into space or hanging around their colleague's door wasting their time YOU will be ready to prospect with fervour to get your candidates excited about the opportunity and will possess the armour when defending against objections and fears of changing careers.

This is a simple exercise but like any physical exercise (like at the gym) it should be applied repeatedly and at slightly different angles to build the most strength. By getting good at this technique, you will have an advantage over your competitors for the best talent and even over your peers for advancement. It's easy and it works for almost any learnable skill or product but we will apply it to recruiting in this section.

From a candidate's perspective, they want three things from you when considering a move from one career to another: succinctness, confidence, and transferability. Brevity recognizes the importance of time, both yours and theirs, as well as demonstrates that you are completely knowledgeable about the subject matter and have no problem talking about it. By not hesitating when high-level questions are asked it shows poise and assurance.

Cover salient points in a shortened form as it is far more likely to be easily communicated between people, especially when that person, a spouse for example, will be affected by the decision of changing careers. Provide candidates the essential facts needed to think about the career opportunity and present those facts in an "infectious" format, meaning it is easily transferable and will stick with the candidate for at least 24 hours.

Here is how it works: think of at least five memorable and important points that support your thesis (whatever topic you chose) that you will present to the other person. For example, to address the question: why should anyone come into the financial industry at this time? Let me give you five reasons to think about on your drive home after our interview:

1. There are two aspects of future life that will be paramount: health and finance. Living as long as possible and having the money to have the best care possible. <u>Our industry is very important</u>.

2. <u>To help protect people in our community</u> and prevent them from outliving their savings. It is important to start planning for estate accumulation, protection, and eventual distribution now.

3. <u>Large inter-generational wealth transfer</u> will happen between the baby boomers and their parents. Over \$1 trillion is going exchange hands in the next 15 years, and we are needed to facilitate this transfer.

4. Traditional employers are reducing benefits and control of career security. It would be good to be paid what you're worth and have <u>a career that can never be taken away from you</u>.

5. <u>There are very low entry costs</u> to get into a white-collar, six-figure income. Similar careers such as lawyers, doctors, or large franchise owners take humungous capital and time.

6. **BONUS POINT:** There are <u>not enough qualified people in our industry now</u> to assist building client's wealth and passing on their estates in a tax-favourable manner. Consider the opportunity when many advisors retire in the next 10 years!

You get the point, and I encourage you to keep building on this list. Write them down. You can do this with any significant aspect, and can brainstorm with your peers. Do this exercise for why someone should join your company or why they should specifically join YOUR branch.

Why should someone join the <u>financial services industry?</u>

1.

2.

3.

4.

5.

Why should someone join <u>your company?</u>

1.

2.

3.

4.

5.

Why should someone join <u>your agency?</u>

1.

2.

3.

4.

5.

Recruiting Mature and Experienced Candidates

Experienced Candidates

This is a double-edged sword to grow your agency; it's ready to use and already sharp. However, you can cut yourself on it accidentally. Let us start with the positive elements first. Any experienced advisor, meaning an agent who has sold financial products for commission for over one year, is someone who survived the dangerous "adolescence" period of our career. They are very realistic about how hard one needs to work to be a successful entrepreneur and are already trained on most products, sales concepts, and business administration. So why are these experienced agents open to having a coffee with you to discuss joining your agency? It is a crucial question and one you need to discover quickly using your instinct and experience. If you don't have these attributes (yet) then I'd strongly recommend bringing along a senior manager.

Sometimes the experienced advisor you are talking to is looking for a better "fit" with their business goals and improved resources of doing business, or perhaps you are geographically closer to their market after they moved into your area, or maybe they appreciated starting their agent career in an organization like yours and now want to bring their son or daughter into the business with your help. Never forget you are the gatekeeper to your organization here. If you feel the candidate's intention is good and they would be an asset then proceed with the selection process and trust that process to do its job.

Often I've found it's that they are missing something from their current organization. Some of the motivators I found are: lack business alignment between what the agent wants to do and what the organization wants them to do; lack of professional development such as tenure roadblocks for attaining a CFP designation; lack the connection to a mentor or coaching manager; lack of recognition; or lack of social attachment with like-minded peers. Let's face it, this can be a lonely and challenging career already but if you're alone it's even more so. At times, it's nice to have some fun and have your family connect with people you spend most of the week with!

The reason to look at changing companies is almost never because of the product suite or client software they're currently using, and it's not usually the people they work with either. It's almost always the environment they are currently in. They want more of something they aren't getting at their current agency. If you have what they need and can express it succinctly and sincerely, you very likely have a good chance of attracting them to your team.

If the vibe you get is that the stated reason to switch companies is not lining up with what you've seen in the resume or heard in the subtext of your conversations together then slow down. It's your choice to gather more information or simply end it there. I've walked away from experienced candidates because I believed they were repeatedly burning through several start-up packages from other reputable competitors such as taking initial signing bonuses or exhausting a base salary provided in the first six months. Are they looking to re-commission clients from their warm market or need a clean start because they burnt bridges with previous organizations or were a compliance concern?

Mature Candidates

I've found the 55-plus markets and even individuals who have entered early retirement can become excellent advisors. A generation or two ago this group would have been called "seniors" and it would have been unthinkable to hire them for their first white-collar role. However, with expanding longevity and the financial realities of living in North America, this group that would traditional retire soon is a great workforce pool that still has 10-20 years of productive career potential ahead of them. Many industries may not give the mature candidate a chance to start a new career because they consider them too old to learn a new role, too costly to hire when they could bring on someone at one-third the age willing to do the job for half the income, or may be concerned at not getting a good rate of return on their investment of time and energy. However, their mistake can be your advantage.

This often-dismissed market will increasingly be a value to our industry and our country's economy for several reasons. Some of the best agents I've worked with are those who have cleaned out their locker, collected their retirement packages, and after a few months of sitting at home, have gotten itchy feet.

I have an amazing agent named Amrik who was a millwright in a logging mill up in Northern BC. After being "retired" for a short amount of time he started to look for a challenge that would allow him to help people and still have flexible time for family. After looking at some options, and not compromising on the next endeavour he would start, he decided to join our office. He qualified for two sales campaigns and convention within six months while showing an enthusiasm and energy that rivals a twenty-year-old. Throughout the last eight years, he has been one of my best partners in growing and supporting the culture of my agency and has become a great friend. We are incredibly lucky to have him and I bet traditional employers would have put his resume in the "B" pile in the HR department.

The mature group is easier to interview because after 40 years in the workforce they know what they like and don't like in a career and in a manager. They will be completely honest with you and are often not under financial pressure to compromise for the sake of a role. If they say they're interested in being an agent with your company, you can believe it. They will not waste your time, or theirs, on idealistic dreams or job interview banter.

They often have great work ethics and have worked for most of their life; they have gotten a few lessons from the schools of hard knocks and have learned to plan for the future. They have visited many friends in hospitals, attended enough funerals, and talked to enough neighbours who are having financial difficulties to know. You don't have to sell them on the importance of protecting assets and family as well as putting money away for unforeseen events.

For many of the baby-boomer generation there will be more of them leaving the workforce at traditional retirement ages only to re-enter it again for different objectives. Unlike their own parents, they are not interested in getting a gold watch and sitting in their reclining chairs waiting for the newspaper to come or the kids to call. They will want to feel productive and have meaningful work that utilizes their hard-won experience and skills. These people may have a decade or more to contribute in an important industry such as ours.

Our roles have no "expiry date"; you can be eighty and still be in the game if your health and enthusiasm remains intact. Who cares if they've got bad knees, it's their brains and ability to connect to people that matters in our occupation. We're not asking them to move pianos or get a medal in the Olympic relay team here. These people have a huge wealth of human experience and are fantastic at dealing with delicate financial situations or angry clients because they have a certain calmness that comes from being around the planet a while.

Mature candidate desire the opportunity to be part of a group that is alive and dynamic again. Certainly financial services have a wide cross-section of ages in men and women still trying to build something versus wind it down. It can be absolutely fantastic for them to feel part of the community that's still valued and contributing, where they can learn, help others, and come home at the end of the day and say to their partner "I made a difference today."

Another significant advantage of this group is that they are not 25-year-olds whose warm markets only buy $20 term products, who feel invincible therefore do not need insurance, or are reluctant to save for the future because they have an eternity to worry about retirement. The mature agent's market oftentimes has significant investments and accumulated properties. Their prospects are more open to plan for retirement and health care needs in the next stage of life. Why? Because they too can see the end-point not too far away and have been exposed to devastating financial situations where the impacts of inaction are clear. Their market is comprised of people who have the ability to pay for permanent insurance products and while it may be more expensive due to their age or less-than-perfect current health, they see the value of paying for these solutions. There comes a trust with an agent who has some gray hair and wrinkles around the eyes who says, "I've worked with people in your situation before and I believe this mixture of products would help put you on the path."

I hope that in the upcoming years more people in this demographic look at this industry and recruiters pay attention to it. It's a niche market that should not be discounted as they have a lot to give, I would recruit a boatload of them if I could. Once contracted with your agency, conduct their training and later coaching session recognizing their life experience and do not treat them like typical rookie agents. Throughout your time working together, talk to them respectfully. Ask them what their expectations are from you or their coaching manager and be clear what you expect for them. After that, let them succeed, they know how.

Remember they are looking for a career they feel would fit their lifestyle now and that they often have the luxury of choice. They know their own weaknesses and strengths. They know how to prioritize and focus on work. While they may not have the distractions of raising children or the pressure of mortgage payments anymore, balancing a career with health and life is very important. Give this mature market a chance to get back in the game; you may be pleasantly surprised finding what your competitors overlooked.

Recruiting within Ethnic Markets

This group of candidates is as diverse as the ethnic markets available: Ukrainian, Korean, Pilipino, South Asian, African, and Chinese just to name a few. Each comes with their own challenges and opportunities, but if you want to tap into an ethnic market in your area of responsibility then you need an advisor who knows the culture and can work effectively within it. If you want to own that ethnic market and have a team of advisors working in a specific community then you need a sales manager from it as well. Some may argue it's not necessary but you will find it a whole lot easier to conduct the training, joint fieldwork, and coaching if the manager is fluent with how the market works.

Depending on their personal motivations, the immigrant market can be one of your best and deepest pools to prospect in. I'm generally speaking about the immigrant market that are newly imported to your country or "first generation" citizens who are largely influenced by their immigrant parents but were actually born in your country. I'm one of those individuals; I was born in Canada but my mother was born in the UK. These brave people took the chance to leave their home country to start anew with very little. The "I can make it" psychology that persists in this market can create ambitious candidates who are near desperate to get on a better career track quickly and to afford the comfortable lifestyle that inspired them to immigrate in the first place.

The challenges people in this group have to overcome are expensive and daunting enough: finding a job, finding a place to live, re-buying furniture, getting kids into new schools, and so on. But what about the intangible things? Not only are they learning a new culture and joining an unfamiliar community but also concurrently trying to retain their cultural identity. Taking on this sort of task speaks volumes about the candidate and the family dynamics they grew up in.

Very often, these people understand what hard work really means and don't take anything for granted. They don't feel entitled to make a good living; they want a chance to have one. Many North Americans in general, despite their original immigrant roots have kind of lost touch after a couple generations here for this drive to succeed and prove they can do it. Too often I hear about unfortunate products of our system where they finish high school, maybe complete a couple of years in college to keep parents off their back then get any job to move out. They make enough to buy stuff and maybe life will sort itself out before age thirty. I see people with their hands off the steering wheel of life, trusting that airbags will deploy if they hit something unsavoury. Time will tell.

A challenge to overcome in the selection process is that the paperwork, textbooks, and exams will not be in their primary language. They will require extra time, training, and coaching to get through these obstacles and be successful. Put yourself in their shoes; how would you feel going to Russia and trying to pass a financial exam?

I was fortunate to be introduced to Ivan, a man with intelligence, drive and past business success in his former country of Brazil before he moved to Canada. He was introduced to me by one of my top senior agents and while he currently held a job he wanted to re-enter a white collar profession. His primary language was Portuguese and therefore had a greater challenge than his peers to get through the licensing exams. I'm proud to say that after 6 years in our agency he is excelling in our career and is a valued friend to me and our agency. I knew he had great capability and the extra time and effort on both our parts was well worth it.

The immigrant market I have had the privilege to work with puts a high value on taking advantage of every situation in North America to further themselves and their families. The will sacrifice much to have an opportunity to send a child to college or join a second family to buy a home. They may have to start again by waiting on tables or stacking boxes in a warehouse but they have ambition and move as fast as possible to new opportunities. I love their pioneer outlook.

We have all heard of people who were doctors or MBAs running engineering companies in their former country but now drive taxis or work in shopping malls selling t-shirts. Their new country unfortunately does not recognize their prior credentials or capabilities and they may not have the resources to pay to re-do their education to re-enter their professional occupation.

Luckily, our industry has very low barriers to joining a white-collar career. For the price of a couple hundred of dollars for textbooks, exams, and first business license, these driven individuals can get into a career where they can get six figures relatively quickly and rebuild an amazing lifestyle. If they wanted to be a dentist or a lawyer, it would cost tens of thousands of dollars and going this route would take years to complete. To join our industry someone can start working and building their business in a matter of months. It sounds good to you right? It sounds even better to the person across the table from you.

Often a second-generation immigrant can see this opportunity. If their parents weren't able to secure good jobs quickly in the last couple of decades then they may not have the opportunity for university or live in a home the family actually owned. We have all seen this unfortunate pattern; some people are able to get out of this track and create a new lifestyle for their family tree. For the right person, if you give them an opportunity they will not squander it.

Immigrant agents are satisfying to coach because they will readily accept feedback. You are a manager from a developed country in a good company within a thriving industry in a position of leadership; don't discount the impression this has on someone willing to learn from you. Show them how to achieve a good income, develop them, and try to understand a bit of their culture and you'll probably have a great agent for a long time. The loyalty that you will find in that market can be outstanding.

Recruiting Single Parents

I have found a good recruiting pool within single parent families. Oftentimes single parents need flexibility of time and control over their incomes. Many times, they are stuck in part-time roles in retail or administration. They take on unconventional or even erratic work schedules because they need to work around their children's timetables. They work over-time and take on co-workers' shifts during the holidays to drive up their income and trade shifts to take off the times they need.

Prior to being single parents they may have been a homemaker or primary care-giver but now through necessity have to re-enter the workforce after an absence or perhaps without needed qualifications. This puts them at a disadvantage when competing for higher-paying full-time jobs. Single parents have to supplement their family's income on top of spousal support or child alimony; simply stated they have to work.

This situation happened to a good friend of mine in her early forties. She worked full-time at a local car dealership as a receptionist and it was very difficult to get ahead. With spousal support and her ability to budget well she was able to ensure her kids attended swimming classes, took family camping vacations, and brought presents to friend's birthday parties, but her income required her to rent a basement suite and she didn't have much to save at the end of each month. From the kids' perspective everything was OK but once they got jobs and left home she didn't have much for herself.

Unfortunately, the kinds of jobs that have the flexibility needed paid very little in our recent economies. I have seen many hard-working single parents earn "poverty line" incomes grinding away at $15/hour for 30 hours a week, making $20,000 or $25,000 annually. This situation can be adequate if they are receiving a significant amount of financial support from the spouse but that doesn't last forever. Sooner or later, they find themselves in a place where they haven't built home equity or accumulated enough savings as their married peers that possess double the household incomes.

Luckily, our industry allows a single parent to build, or rebuild, their income track and provides the essential time flexibility to juggle family and client demands. If they started as an agent on a part-time basis to begin with, they can develop their practise steadily as the kids become more self-sufficient. If they started as a full-time financial advisor right from the start, because they can work 40 hours every week just not in a row. Over the next 10-15 years as the kids become independent, the single parent will now have grown a substantial income and own a fully operational business practise.

Recruiting into this market has provided me with a chance to work with some outstanding people over my 12 years. They appreciate the opportunity and have proven to me many times over the arrangement can really work. They describe a typical day: drop kids off at school at 8:15 a.m. then get home or to the office at 9:00 a.m., do their prospecting calls and appointment confirmations, arrange business quotes, and pre-fill paper work before lunchtime. They can arrange appointments with individuals and business owners that appreciate daytime meetings then they pick up the kids from school, have dinner and some family time. Sometimes, as needed, they get a family member or babysitter to watch younger children while evening appointments are done. They often create a professional home office to have clients come to them, which maximizes work time while minimizing commuting.

Oftentimes the hardest part with having single parent agents is getting them in the agency for structured training and weekly coaching. Since they may not always be able to attend normal coaching and development schedules within the branch, obviously, you wouldn't want to make an entire branch based on this type of market but a reasonable percentage can be accommodated comfortably without too much strain on your trainers. Another great advantage to this group is that many single parents happen to be connected to other single parents. If you can create a few success stories and change the lives of agents that come from this demographic, you will get strong candidate referrals. The pros have outweighed the cons in the past; I encourage you to try targeting this market as a viable recruiting opportunity.

Our industry looks to more on what a candidate can do versus what they have done; this is a weakness in other occupations but is a strength for us.

Traditional employers often say, "I can see in your resume that in the last two years you've had three secretarial jobs." Often this can limit the interviewer's vision of the candidate capabilities. Many employers I have talked to say that if they see repetitive occupation history on a resume they assume this is what the person is capable of doing or all they want to do. This is an understandable heuristic: when the HR department has ninety applications for a job posting they use simple filter strategies to categorize applicants quickly. They are usually not thinking, "This person may not fit the job we're filling today but I bet with their ambition and interest in trying a new career path we could spend a year to develop them into something amazing." That doesn't happen out there, but it does with our industry.

I often try to coach candidates I interview that may not be a fit for my agency but have potential for a greater career than they are currently experiencing. At least try to get them into an industry with growth potential because sooner or later their tired resume will pigeonhole them into a damaging job-track. Virtually no employer will take them seriously if they say they are capable of a white-collar profession but their resume shows a dozen years in a local cosmetic department. We'll take a chance where other companies can't or won't.

Recruiting Women Agents

For every market you wish to prospect within you need to determine what motivates them and what elements they are looking for in their next career move. To attract them, to coach them after contracted, and to retain them effectively later you should continually address these points once identified. These points are their career-drivers or, potentially, deal breakers in changing careers. A lot will come through the selection process. They might be aware of the source of their discomfort and statements may come to you in the form of "micro-management in my current job drives me crazy" or "I could keep everything else in my job but I don't feel challenged." Sometimes the candidates honestly don't know but they feel capable of more in life or should at least be paid more for what they do. Perhaps they are feeling content about their current situation but came to your office curious to learn more. Whatever the reason, they got in their car and drove across town to spend an hour with you; therefore, there is some opportunity to pique their interest. This is your window; make the most of it.

Whether this information is volunteered by the candidate or it's something you have to tenaciously dig out, learning what is motivating and what is not allows you to offer a solution. In the initial meeting, I routinely ask the question "If you had a magic wand, how would you create a perfect career for yourself?" or "Paint me a picture of what you really want in your next career" or even approach the antithesis of their dream role "Describe for me three things you really don't want in your next career opportunity." Then shut up, listen, and take notes.

The current workforce pool is 50 percent female and a big recruiting opportunity available to us. Whether it's politically correct to say it or not, I have found that women are generally attracted to careers, stay in careers, change careers, excel in careers, or fail in careers for different reasons than men. North American males had traditionally made up the majority of workers, and that percentage in financial services is no different. Over hundreds of years of enterprise, various workplaces have figured out how to motivate, communicate, coach, develop, and retain men. However, since World War II, women have entered into the workforce in every role imaginable and have certainly shown they can do any career that men can.

Prospecting in the "women's market" can be largely divided into two categories: those already in the workforce, and those returning to the workforce. In the financial industry, women make up only about one third of agents and less than a quarter in sales management positions. The reasons for this after years of equal opportunities for women are hard to accurately state, and can be hotly argued from different academic disciplines, but we will not delve into the debate here. Women are a minority in an industry that remains largely middle-aged Caucasian males. Since it's an under-represented and developing market segment, it's therefore a valid recruiting opportunity.

Female advisors are often attracted to advisor careers, sometimes for different reasons than men, and they certainly desire to be trained and coached once on board, but those divergent reasons change the way you find them and how you recruit them. The women I've interviewed and worked with over a twelve year span have been more interested in time flexibility, interacting with people, earning an income based on performance criteria identical to their male peers, and meaningful work that positively impacts others in their local community.

Many of the "systems" of training and coaching used by traditional corporations often use a cookie-cutter approach to managing their people and unfortunately our industry doesn't fare much better in this regard. I believe that this half of the potential workforce does not excel by using the exact same tools used for male workers, or commissioned agents for that matter.

Generally, I found that men have a desperate need to belong and to be accepted by a group. Whether it's joining the military or Cub Scouts, or a pack of boys kicking a ball in the street they want to be invited and be part of a group they can take pride in. They are "pack-oriented" and since there is an identity that comes with belonging, they likely won't do anything to jeopardize that involvement and affiliation.

At the end of the day, despite social advancements and workplace politics, men derive their "value" from their role to have an occupation. No matter whether they are single or married with kids, having a career is a large part of their identity; work often equals identity. Further, real or perceived success at work equates with success in life. Whether having a company car, a corner window office, or a six-figure income to brag about, the traditional workplace structures have learned how to appeal to men's thinking and regularly use these strategies to retain or pull them from one company to the other.

Comparatively, for many women their identity and feeling of success in life is not wrapped up in what they do for 40 hours a week. It's often not what they are. Therefore, when competing in the workforce pool you must have a different approach to attract them to your agencies. For example, a man may become interested in moving to another company because of a $5,000 income increase whereas a woman might move based on the opportunity to have a better quality of life or doing a more meaningful job.

As long as a man can wield a shovel or stack boxes in a warehouse, he can probably get employment somewhere; his base skill is labour. For women it's often service work whether hospitality, retail, or caregiver roles. Women also re-enter the workforce after long absences for reasons such as after raising children or a divorce. The traditional workforce opportunities often penalize them at this time, and regardless of what level they were at before their absence they now have to "reset" their careers and start at the bottom. There is a massive opportunity within our industry because we don't care what you've done, or how long you haven't been doing it; we're more concerned with what you might yet be able to do.

To reiterate, men want to belong to a successful team where they gain respect and the chance to move up the rankings in a group so for men you can emphasize points like a winning culture, development, and how you treat top achievers. Talk about the best agents in your agency and how they too can belong to a special cadre if their performance is good enough (like qualifying for MDRT). If they are title-motivated, you can relate how your agency helps them achieve accreditations and designations. In an initial meeting, how they do or do not react to such information can be very telling.

On the other hand, keeping women agents engaged in their role often means appreciation of and connection to the agency (as well as relationships). Inquire into what happens in a current typical day for the candidate to learn how a flexible work schedule would be beneficial. Discover their obligations and commitments and how their current occupation is not addressing this properly. Find out exactly what their hot buttons are. Women can be just as income motivated and recognition driven, but for possibly different reasons.

Conducting an Initial Interview

Essentially the selection process works through face-to-face interviews. There can certainly be more meetings to cover additional tasks required, such as proprietary sign-offs for your company, reviewing relevant homework, or assisting the candidate in preparing for licensing exams. What I'm speaking about are the mandatory structured interviews done between a recruiting manager and a potential candidate. Obviously there are many steps involved in choosing the right candidate for success in the industry, but of particular significance are the four structured interviews completed between a manager and a candidate.

A very time-efficient and arguably the most important meeting of the selection process is the initial interview; at the end of which you decide if you want to move ahead with the candidate and they decide if you'll get a second interview. The initial interview really shouldn't be called an "interview" as it is more of a casual conversation. It is a chance for a potentially interested person to meet with somebody in the industry for a brief description of the position and have their initial questions and concerns answered. What is an advisor? What is your company about? Why would you have considered me? Usually this get-together is no more than 30 minutes long and can be held either at the organization or branch's location, or off-site at a coffee shop or hotel lounge.

The advantage of having the initial interview at your business location is it allows the candidate to see the potential working environment, the professionalism of the office as well as have a chance to informally meet other advisors and staff who are there at the time. Earlier I mentioned that the meeting could be in the office or outside of it. An additional advantage of having the initial interview in the office that's worth considering is the fact that if the candidate is unable to attend (stuck in traffic, mixed up the date, car broke down, or just doesn't show at all!) you can continue to be productive at the agency until your next candidate arrives. If you feel you have a strong contender, you have the tools at hand to illustrate a point, take them on a tour of the office or introduce them to an advisor in the office you think they would connect well with.

The advantage of meeting somewhere more relaxed is it reflects the informal nature of the "interview" and puts the potential candidate more at ease. It can also be a great way to see the "real" person versus the upright posture of a formal interview! There is no "right" or "wrong" location; it is best decided by considering the person you are meeting. If they are a candidate that has little understanding of the career and are a bit puzzled why they were even approached, a less formal surrounding would likely be more appropriate.

From a candidate's point of view, it's about getting their initial questions answered before they step further into the official selection process. It is crucial that you answer those initial questions they have, or they will not journey with you any farther down the path of exploring the career. Subsequently, start off the meeting asking what questions they need answered before concluding the meeting. What do they want to know? Sometimes their questions will drive most of the time allotted, and that's not a bad thing. At the end of the meeting, they will shake hands and jump either into the selection process or out of it.

From your point of view, you want to meet and screen as many potential candidates as you can each week because a good portion of whom you meet will not make it through the selection process. Bottom line: the initial interview allows you to ensure that your time is going to be spent dealing only with those candidates who have the potential and enthusiasm to go further without having to give up a lot of your time, or theirs.

Although you want to make sure the meeting is answering their questions, there are a couple of key items you need to know early on to save you both grief later one: 1) Are they entitled to work in your country? 2) Does the candidate foresee any difficulty in passing a background checks and obtaining a license? There is nothing more disheartening for everyone concerned if weeks into the selection process, with licensing books purchased and hours of study completed, that you discover your candidate has an impaired driving conviction or declared bankruptcy and won't be eligible to join the organization no matter how wonderful you think they are. Save everyone pain and ask those two questions right away.

If you have the resume either prior to the interview or given to you during it, take the time to read and review it and allow it to paint a picture for you of the person's habits, look at addresses and business employment over the last 10 years.

Also take a look at what type of work is indicated. If they are working in retail or restaurants, they are probably good at working with people or the public as long as they are in sales, rather than administration. Titles of businesses or employers can be an income indicator. Sometimes it's good information to know what income level this person is living with, or something that might be frustrating them. Are there gaps in the work history, anything unexplained as to why they weren't making money? A trained manager should be able to review all of these things and formulate questions for them within 30 seconds.

After gaining a quick understanding of the person's resume, look at the candidate and if you perceive somebody whose potential is beyond what you're seeing in the resume, you may have someone who is frustrated in their current career. If you look at the resume and it matches the person, perhaps the person is actually in the career they should be in. The more concrete information you get during the interview the easier it will be for you to select or deselect candidates. It has been said when it comes to human career performance the best predictor of tomorrow's behaviour is past behaviour. By listening and documenting their history of effort, success, development, and energy, you will have a better chance at picking a great candidate. Tell the candidate that you will be taking notes, and be sure to present yourself as an avid listener.

Give them enough time to answer your questions, and don't coach them in their responses. Sometimes silence is the best things you can do for a candidate while they are trying to think of their answer. It may feel uncomfortable but respect the time the candidate needs to give you an honest answer. Make sure you appear interested by demonstrating you are listening, and the easiest way to demonstrate that is to paraphrase their responses or their answers to you. And lastly, where you need more information, don't be afraid to probe further into the concern; your instinct may guide you to the reason that this candidate may be unsuitable. Trust your instincts; that's what they're there for, to tell you if you are walking into trouble.

The Initial Interview

At the very beginning of what could be a long working relationship it is important to give yourself and the candidate permission to not proceed. Agree that if you both decide to move ahead then you will set up the next meeting. However, if either one of you thinks this is not a good fit at this time, it's OK to move ahead. You can explicitly say to the candidate "you have my commitment that if I feel this is not a good fit, I will tell you we should postpone the process and I'm asking the same commitment of you today. I'm OK with a 'no thank you' and any decision to move ahead will be a mutual one, does that sounds fair?" It's just good business; if the candidate is uncomfortable, we cannot move ahead and, if we are uncomfortable then give yourself permission to professionally stop the process.

After sitting the candidate down and providing a notepad, pen, and a glass of water bring out a blank piece of paper. Draw a vertical line down the middle of the page. On the left hand side, capture what the candidate says is important to them in an ideal career opportunity as well as items they do not want to have in their next position. On the right hand side of the vertical line, match up what is important to them and what your organization offers. At the end of the meeting, you should have 5 to 10 components of what they want on the left, with corresponding points of how your agency addresses and fulfils those components. It's just that easy!

Some great queries to ask throughout the interview are "thinking questions" posed for the candidate. Oftentimes experienced candidates are familiar with conventional HR interviewing techniques and become quote "polished" in the answer. A question like "what do you like about your current job" doesn't dig deep enough. So if you have a good candidate, put them on the spot saying "Mr. Candidate, let's assume you are selected by our agency, let us also assume you pass the licensing requirements to become a financial advisor in July. If we go forward one year from then and you are an unsuccessful advisor, why do you think that would be?"

It may take a long while, and it's important to remain silent at this point, but the answer given will likely be accurate. I've heard responses like "I'm unable to build a market." Or "I may not be able to influence people to decide to place business with me" or "I'm unable to balance work and family life" and so on. Because they know themselves better than you know them at this point, take stock in their answers because their answers will likely tell you their biggest obstacle in choosing this career. You could also flip the question and ask, "Can you give me three reasons why you think you would be a successful financial advisor?"

It is always important to document their responses, write down the questions that they think are important as well as details of some of their responses. If you are moving ahead with the candidate, this will be important to bring you back to the same headspace you were in before starting the meeting. If you and the candidate decide not to move ahead, having the notes will be beneficial to include with the follow-up letter that is sent to their home. In the letter, provide details on what to overcome or something you would like to see if they want to apply for the position in the future. Keep a copy of any letter you send. It has happened to me more than once; somebody calls me a year later saying they are interested at looking at the role again and I had difficulty remembering who that person was. By looking at the name and filed letter, I am able to catch up and continue the conversation professionally.

Stay in Touch

When following up with the candidate during the selection process, do not let 48 hours go by without you or one of your managers connecting with them. I recommend that managers and their assistants have a system so as to not re-think every time a common situation comes up. For example, if it's a successful initial interview and both parties have agreed to move to a more formal meeting next time, have a previously created package of information ready. This tangible package is for the candidate (and perhaps their spouse) to read and digest, perhaps with their spouse, between now and the next meeting. I always include information about my company, my agency's story, and a one-page biography about me. We may work closely together later, so they should know my business philosophy as well as who I am as a person. I also recommend connecting candidates to your LinkedIn profile.

I also include objective, third-party information such as articles from public newspapers in the industry or opportunities in the agent's role. Sometimes I even include the third-party information on the challenges too. We could give them specific packages that target certain groups like female markets, ethnic markets, and experienced licensed candidates. By having prepared kits or a system for doing these things, you eliminate the thinking involved when you try to coordinate the next meeting.

Further, the period of time between an initial interview and the comprehensive meeting is another opportunity to establish a connection with the candidate as well as provide them with more information. After a gap of several days, they will be able to receive and digest this information, which may peak their interest in the position. Being old fashioned, I like sending letters to make an impression. During the day a text or email works well as a quick follow up but with people absorbing 100 messages a day it has lost much of its impact. Some people check their email less than every two days and the younger generation may check it once a week. It is more professional and impactful to receive a well-worded letter on good-quality paper.

In a time where applicants don't expect to receive professional letters from a potential employer, sending one to their home leaves an indelible mark on their thoughts until you meet again (see Candidate Welcome Letter example). Not only will this give an impact to the candidate upon coming back to their mailbox, but the letter will have an impact on their spouse too. When they pick up the mail and say, "Honey, we received a letter from the big company you interviewed with last week, they must be very interested in you." This will generate a conversation between them and you may find more detailed questions come up during the formal meeting. Additionally, in these letters I send I can also include materials specifically pertinent to the candidate.

If you are working in an ethnic market like our agency does, include testimonials in your letter from successful advisors from the ethnic community your candidate identifies with. Find an appropriate article that speaks about how their ethnic markets are highly prosperous in our industry and put that in as well. Not only will it impact the candidate it will also impact everyone in their household.

However, if the initial interview was not successful and for the time being no future formal meeting was set, there is still an opportunity to place an importance on the time spent together in the initial meeting as well as potentially keeping the door open for that person in a specific amount of time like six months. I still believe that in this situation a professional letter sent to the home is a very good practise. Even if both of you agree it's not the best idea to move ahead at this time, a professional letter makes a big difference to the candidate in whether the candidate will be positive in returning through your doors again in the future.

Comprehensive Meeting (with or without VIP)

Whereas the first interview is meant to initially screen or engender interest in a career opportunity in a candidate's mind, I view these meetings as off the record conversation. There's no obligation either way between me and the candidate to go further. However, after the initial meeting has gone well and both I and the candidate are comfortable exploring in more detail what this opportunity looks like then the comprehensive meeting will proceed with more in-depth questions. These structured questions need to directly probe the candidate's ability to develop a market, their comfort with sales as a career, and set expectations on first year incomes. At the same time, ask preliminary questions regarding their criminal and credit status as well take a closer look at the individual's integrity and potential business plan.

Some larger scale organizations have developed scripted questions and have focused topic points to ensure specific areas are addressed. As managers in such organizations, we need to follow these booklets or interview guidelines to the best of our ability but I believe that it is our responsibility in meetings to ask additional questions to determine the suitability of the candidate within our own branch and community. As I like to say, the structure given can be considered the black and white lines within which a good field manager can ask the colorful questions that make a complete picture.

Initially I start out with comfortable questions that get candidates used to talking about themselves preferably on topics of which they are proud or enthusiastic. I found that a great way to ensure getting details is to start with the phrase "paint me a picture of" or "tell me a story about" a particular topic. For example, tell me a story about a class you enjoyed in university or paint me a picture of an ideal career for you in the next five years. This gets the candidate thinking about positive things and makes them less defensive on the more probing questions later such as their strategies for success.

If you believe the candidate is comfortable in talking about their past employment, it is a good idea to learn what the candidate liked and disliked about previous roles. Certainly, it is a good idea on any of these points to probe a little bit deeper if there are any red flags in their comments. Sometimes I ask them to describe a great manager or supervisor they've had in their past, to understand what type of style they react best to. Inevitably, the reverse of this question is brought up by the candidate to mention the worst manager or director they've had over the years. Again it's a great opportunity to learn why.

This phase of the interview process is to learn as much about the person as possible; if you feel there were any gaps in the initial interview, this is the time to ask. Ask them about hobbies and interests they are passionate about, how much time they spend on these activities, and why they started these hobbies. The type of activity will tell you if the individual is more introspective such as reading books, more social such as leading group activities or hiking with others, or more team-minded such as competitive sports like volleyball or hockey.

Make sure you ask the candidate "what is their definition of success." In the past, I have heard comments about income figures, weeks of vacation, number of properties accumulated, job security, peer awards, living a significant life, etc. Also ask them about instances when they felt most successful and to tell you a story about that.

From any of these above points it is critical to make notes as it will allow you to paraphrase back to them the meaningful things that were told to you. The goal of any interview is to determine if the candidate feels that you understand who they are, what their situation is, and a little bit about their hopes and dreams. If the candidate feels that you understand these things and have the opportunities that will address those things, they are most likely to follow through the selection process.

Depending on how well this interview goes, I often close with one of two questions. If I believe the candidate is truly a good fit for my branch and the industry, I will end with a question, "What is the number one reason why you would be successful in a career with us if I were able to make an offer?" From here, I have had candidates spend the last ten minutes of the meeting selling me on why they would be fantastic in their career, why their hearts are in the right place to be an advisor, and why they think they are capable of being an advisor. Essentially the meeting is wrapped up by the candidate "closing themselves" into the next step of the selection process.

If, however, I have concerns about the candidate, I will ask the reverse of this question, "If I were to offer you a role in the company as an agent and you are able to successfully join our branch but several years from now you are unsuccessful and had to leave the business, for what reason would you think that would have happened?" This too has revealed very enlightening comments from the candidate. Statements such as not having enough people to talk to, not being able to close the sale, not being able to balance work and family, and so on.

It has been my experience that the candidate has accurate unconscious assessments of themselves, and they are often right to pause. Oftentimes, candidates like these save both of us time by de-selecting themselves in light of their own admitted weaknesses. If they do come back, I address those self-identified points to ensure we are both comfortable that coaching and training can overcome those problems.

Throughout the interview process I want to hear about instances where their character was tested such as how they dealt with a conflict of interest, what they did if they saw a colleague being dishonest, how they handled a tough client or customer situation, how they assisted family members in a time of crisis, or how they coped with a divorce. Hearing about how the candidate proactively became involved in solving problems, counselling other people, and accomplishing tasks in difficult situations are important indicators of some of the skills and behaviours that will be needed to be a successful advisor.

Moreover, asking questions that determine work ethic are also a clue into the person sitting across the table from you. Asking the candidate if they worked at the same time as going through high school or post-secondary shows me an ability to manage time and effort with multiple deadlines. Also, get them to explain situations where they had to work longer or harder to be able to successfully complete objectives that were important to them. And this can take the shape of working full-time job while going through the immigration process or working two jobs at the same time due to a disabled spouse.

If I think the candidate has potential as a future field manager, I will ask additional questions that focus on whether or not they have taught a subject to a group, done presentations, or helped other people accomplish goals that were significant to that individual. Asking them for examples of when they were able to gather support for an initiative they wanted to complete or even a large-scale community event is important to discover if they have the ability to inspire others and lead groups to a common goal.

It is also crucial to determine if candidates are able to learn and apply vast amount of information, digest it then explain it to others simply and effectively. This is essentially what financial advisors do all the time. It is our job to understand how investment and insurance products work, federal budget and tax changes, or strategies to pay off mortgages faster. However, the clients that our advisors speak to are understandably not experts in these topics. So the ability to take complex or technical concepts and explain them in a manner that another human being can understand after a long day of work and taking care of kids after dinner is pivotal. The ideas we share have to be clear and concise and for us to do that well we have to understand the concepts in far more detail to ensure that the important parts are covered.

As a decision to change careers is significant and may affect many people in the candidate's household, it is important to include the other decision makers that are part of the candidate's world. This normally takes the form of a spouse, who obviously has a vested interest in the success of the candidate but may also have their own insights and apprehensions that should be heard by the recruiting manager. Sometimes the VIP that I invite to these comprehensive interviews is a good friend, a mentor figure, a professor, or a former employer of the candidate, anyone the candidate trusts.

Additional people at this stage of the selection process can be seen by a new manager as yet another person to convince with more objections to handle, but I think it is a huge opportunity to gain more insight about the candidate. But it is also important to know the environment that this future advisor will be going back to and asking for support and encouragement when you are not around.

For example, after a morning of training sessions and coaching a new recruit prospects and has sales appointments in the afternoon and evening. When they eventually go home and encounter a less-than-positive reaction to how they spent their day, it can undermine what they are trying to do. Hours of positive support from the agency per week cannot compete with hours of negativity in the home environment. If the spouse or VIP truly believes that candidate is not able to do the job, it's important to listen to that person for areas of concern you might have missed. However, if the spouse is fully supportive of a career change for the candidate, they will appreciate the opportunity to be part of the decision and that could provide the basis for a long-term relationship with the spouse for future opportunity for growth.

Topics that are usually a concern for the VIP or spouse are compensation and benefits, the time needed to build a successful career and what impacts changing to career opportunity may have on the household. This makes sense of course because the ability to earn an income to support themselves as well as the ongoing health and relationship of the candidate with their family is of prime concern for the VIP. And it should be for the manager as well if you are looking for a long-term member for your team. Asking open-ended questions to the VIP and keeping a flexible agenda is important in these meetings as it really should be the VIP and the candidate that drive the outcome of this meeting.

As an administrative point, these comprehensive interview steps can be held to either one day or multiple meetings broken up over a course of weeks. During these times, it is recommended you do concurrent activities and complete paper work to be the most efficient with your time and theirs. For example, when the candidate comes in for the comprehensive interview include time to review their reference checks or for a VIP interview you could ask the spouse to assist filling out the market identification booklets. I find the most effective meetings are held in 90 minutes or less. This allows not only you to remain sharp but keeps the energy of the candidate up as well. For the sake of practicality, if it is hard to schedule time together or there is a considerable travel distance between the candidate and the branch, you may have to set up longer meetings that achieve multiple aims.

In my experience, any homework that is given to a candidate to be done between meetings will only get completed if there is follow-up by the manager between meetings. I find a lot of managers that give out business planning workbooks or market surveys, product information to study, and so on in an effort to leverage time may find that they would have to dedicate additional time to ensure the candidate gets the work done. This is not because the candidate is lazy or doesn't see that it is important but as soon as they leave your office, they are immediately thrown back into their regular lives where things can get busy and unexpected distractions may stop them from completing the task you gave them.

Remember, at this point they don't work for you, they work for another employer. The candidate is learning and studying for a new role on top of their social and family commitments. As a manager, if you feel you are doing all the work to make sure that these tasks get done that is a warning sign. Even the most diligent of us do require a friendly nudge from a good friend to go to the gym once in a while even if we know it's for our own good and we enjoy it.

Be a Student of Other Commissioned Roles

I have found it very useful when competing for talent to know your adversary. If you find something attractive in the resume of the person sitting in your interviewing room then chances are someone else does too.

Over the years, I have made it a personal hobby to learn the commission systems of a wide range of occupations. I do this not only to learn what is "fair" in pay for performance roles and to measure how my agent's income stacks up against others, but also to better arm myself in what will eventually be a showdown between what we have to offer as a financial agent versus the other occupation they are looking at (and could even be currently interviewing for).

Each one of the charts below cover the common components that a candidate compares my agency against when making a decision. I try to be as fair as possible in representing the other role and often I let the candidate take it with them after our compensation meeting to show to their spouse to discuss.

In all of the comparisons, I have used at least two credible sources in each specific industry to get my information. These are my COIs and good friends in each of these industries and on big career showdowns I have even sent my candidate to speak with them directly. I value and trust these peers and we routinely refer candidates back and forth if the candidate we are speaking with would be a better fit at their organization than ours. That is just good business.

As these charts are accurate and based on the companies that are in my city and may not be accurate for you city or country, I would encourage you to use these examples as a springboard to create your own comparison charts for the sales careers you find your agency competing against for good agent talent.

Good candidates are often checking out a variety of new career opportunities, not just yours. Be ready for their questions as they will want to compare and contrast the pros and cons of different careers. If you are prepared to fairly and objectively compare the opportunity at your agency against the other company then you will have a distinct advantage.

Do your homework in your own backyard. I have created several "quick reference" sheets for a range of commissioned sales roles we often come across in my city. As a new competitor is brought up by my candidate I take notes and later call a colleague I have in that industry to give me their "selling points" when offering a position. I will then put it into a comparison table and at our next meeting walk the candidate through it. You may not win every situation but you will win a lot more if you're prepared.

Career Comparison – Realtor and Agent Role

	Realtor	Agent at our Office
Licensing Course and First Year Fees	$1300 Real Estate	$600 Insurance $600 Wealth
1st year and 4th year retention	80% / 30%	90% / 70%
Monthly Business Expenses	$250 - $500 if renting office	$300 if renting office
Residual income from client block retained	No, you have to keep selling houses	Yes, paid *every month* the client is retained
Commission	Selling Agent receives $17k on $500k home then pays Buying agent $8k	Typical sale generates $1500 lump sum with $10 monthly trailer
Average income @ 4th year	$100,000	$119,000
Annual Marketing expenses (website, advertisements, packages, etc)	10-15% of annual income	No
Expenses paid to the 'house' for use of brand and local office name	$10-18k per year	None
Career Progression	No	Yes
Training and mentoring provided	No	Yes
Marketing materials provided	No, and there are large advertising costs	Yes
Benefits and Retirement Package	No	Yes
Working hours per week	60+ on-call 24/7	40 hours, flexible
# sales per month to earn $3,500 commission	1	4 insurance sales at $80 premium each
Signing Bonus and establishment account	No	$7,000
Walk-ins, Leads, Reward Travel and Campaign prizes	Very little	Yes
Signing bonus and establishment account	No	$7,000

Career Comparison – Mortgage Broker and Agent Role

	Mortgage Specialist	Agent at our Office
Licensing Course and First Year Fees	$2,000	$600 Insurance $600 Wealth
1st year and 4th year retention	80% / 30%	90% / 70%
Monthly Business Exenses	$300 - $500 if renting office	$300 if renting office
Residual income from client block retained	No	Yes
Can incorporate and have assistants?	No	Yes
Commission	A $250k mortgage yields $1,600 commission, no residual income	$100/mo premium yields $1,300 lump sum plus $10/mo residual income
Average income @ 4th year	$80,000	$119,000
Career Progression	Little unless starting own business	Yes
Marketing materials provided	No	Yes
Benefits and Retirement Package	No	Yes
Working hours per week	50 hours	50 hours flexible
# sales per month to make $3,500	4 mortgages closed	4 insurance calls
Signing Bonus and establishment account	No	$7,000
Compliance Team provided for your protection	No	Yes
1 year of Training and mentoring provided	No	Yes

Career Comparison – Car Dealership Sales Role and Agent Role

	Domestic Car Dealerships	Import Car Dealerships	Agent at our Office
Licensing Course and First Year Fees	$700 VSA	$700 VSA	$600 LLQP
1st year and 4th year retention	25% / 15%	40% / 30%	90% / 70%
Monthly Business Exenses	$200/mo fees	$200/mo fees	$300 for office
Residual income from client block retained	No	No	Yes
Write-off business expenses	No	No	Yes
Commission	21% - 24% of gross profit	30% - 35% of gross	100% of annual premium
Average income 4th year	$60,000 full-time	$70,000 full time	$119,000
Typical commission per sale	$30,000 car sale = $450 lump sum	$30,000 car sale = $600 lump sum	$100/mo premium yields $1,300 lump sum plus $10 *every month*
Career Progression and Development	No	No	Yes
Training and mentoring provided	No	Some	Yes
Benefits and Retirement Package	No	No	Yes
Working hours per week	40 hours min on floor, will take more	40 hours min on floor, will take more	40 hours flexible
# sales per month to make $3,500	8 - 10 new sales or 5 - 6 used car sales	8 - 10 new sales or 5 - 6 used car sales	4 insurance sales
Signing bonus and establishment account	$500 sometimes	$1,000	$7,000

Having a Compensation and Benefits Meeting

By this point you have a screened candidate and perhaps even had opportunities to determine fit and understand their markets. Assuming you find the candidate desirable to have in your agency it is now time to "pivot" the direction of the selection process so the candidate can decide whether to join your organization. Like it or not, it is their belief in being able to earn enough income in this new career opportunity that will largely determine if they will proceed further. At the end of the day, despite many other influences, motivators, and even their VIP's input, the decision will often come down to compensation.

Every organization has a slightly different compensation structure. All of them have strengths and weaknesses and these are normal and natural; however, your job is to present your compensation structure in a way that addresses what the candidate says is important to them as well as how they view their business will develop. It is a natural tendency to only address the components of your company's compensation structure that would make the candidate choose your organization. However, I do find the more holistic and honest you are with them in this meeting about how your compensation structure compares to other structures, the more it will allow the candidate to accurately determine whether or not they choose you.

To believe that a candidate is not looking at other companies now that their eyes have been opened to the opportunity of our industry is dangerous. By addressing multiple models along with yours in even-handed way will accomplish two aims. It will boost your credibility and expertise in the eyes of the candidate and it will also assist them in deciding for themselves which model best suites them. If it's your organization, they will never look over their shoulder for a missed opportunity. If it's not your organization, you have saved both of you a lot of time and frustration before they decide to go to a competitor anyway. You can never go wrong by doing what is in the best interest of the candidate and at this meeting that means fairly and clearly explaining how the candidate can achieve their income objectives with your organization.

I usually start my compensation meeting with three income scenarios. It is important that these are realistic for your branch and geographic location and not to use national averages for incomes, which are clearly not applicable to every corner of the country. You can also take into consideration what they have told you about their market and desired product offerings and adjust these incomes accordingly. For example, for a candidate who says they are going to focus on new homeowners and mortgage insurance markets, I would lower the expected incomes, whereas someone whose working in the 40-something market interested in permanent and critical illness insurance along with retirement planning, I would increase the average.

For my office in Surrey, BC, the average expected income for a first year advisor is about $60,000 with a third year average income of $90,000. All things being equal I usually assume that they are well-rounded advisors selling life and health products and are developing their wealth and group benefits markets but have not become masters yet. I explain below average income is $45,000-$60,000 and this is still above the lower mainland BC average income as reported by the provincial government. I tell the candidate the average income is when they focus on life health and wealth, of course, but also developing a group benefits market as well as peripheral financial sales such as disability and travel insurance. All these income streams will increase their annual income. An above average income is $60,000-$75,000 in the first year and it is obviously a goal for the right candidate with a good market to be trained and coached to this level.

A question I inevitably get from the candidate is if it is possible to make six figures in the first year. I smile and say absolutely but usually they tend to be in the top 20 percent of the rookie advisors but is certainly not the average. It is important to be realistic with a candidate about what income will likely be because if we are both working from a hypothetical and fantasy point of view, if this does not become realized, they will walk down to your office for an unpleasant meeting. As we all know, incomes are unlimited but as the manager and coach for this candidate your credibility is tied to what you think you can do with this candidate at this stage. Like an athlete asking their coach if it is it possible for them to win a gold medal in the Olympics, the answer is yes but it takes time and a lot of work to get there but it is what the athlete brings as part of their talent that will largely determine how great they will be.

Next, I explain the transition often seen in the initial years that changes from a purely insurance-sales-based practise to a more well-rounded one that includes investments and group benefits. Under five years in the business, most of an advisor's income comes from insurance-based sales. It pays the most commission upfront and often has the products that they are allowed to sell without being licensed in additional areas.

Generally, 75 percent of all income in the early years will come from insurance sales with the remaining 25 percent accounting for investments, annuities, health and dental plans, as well as group benefits. Between five and ten years in the business, I see most advisors develop a more holistic business where half of their income comes from insurance production and the other half comes from the investment trailer commissions and group benefits commissions from a now substantial block of business. Over ten years in the business, even with the same individual insurance production, it will be the trailer and group benefits commissions that will overtake the income experienced by the advisor.

It is important to explain an individual sale in an easy to understand manner but to remain scalable. For example, rather than getting into all the different types of commissions and bonuses for a wide range of insurance sales, I would explain an average insurance sale that the candidate can comprehend and more importantly be able to explain later that day to their VIP. This is especially important to the candidate without any commission sales experience that works on an hourly rate. They simply will not understand what income could be generated from one sale.

Early on in the meeting, I will ask the candidate a question that will go something like this: "Mr. Candidate, for a $1,200 annual sale (that is the annual total of "$100 month premium the client pays), what percentage of that sale do you think we give to the agent?" Then you sit back and you listen to their best guess, which inevitably will start low like 20 percent or 30 percent of the annual premium. Their eyes always get bigger as I keep telling them to go higher until we get to the 100 percent and more range. When I explain that for a $1,200 premium sale they could earn over $1,500 in commissions candidates are surprised and sceptical at first. After explaining our compensation system in more detail, they come to understand. However, on the drive home from your office they will start to dream of what is possible with the compensation model you have explained. As part of their thinking, they will start using multiples of your sales examples to estimate what they need to do to achieve their desired annual income.

Similarly for the investment side of the business, walk through an example of a sale with the same approach of a scalable transaction. For example, a $100,000 investment purchase at 3.3 percent DSC equals $3,300 now in upfront commissions with a $30 a monthly trailer. If the same transaction is done on a front-end load schedule, it would be a $70 a month trailer. Again, this is to get the candidate thinking and dreaming of what they could do for an investment activity in their first year and to incorporate that in their realistic income plan.

For your specific organization, make sure you introduce and clearly explain any bonuses or safety systems in your compensation structure. For example, signing bonus upon contract, minimum monthly base income, short-term bonuses, or sales activity for rookies. Make sure they understand. Develop an initial six-month plan to attain as many "wins" as possible as well as introduce any long-term bonus structures such as one or two-year bonuses paid by your organization.

Despite any other interviews that we've done or workbooks or paperwork required for the selection process, this meeting, in the eyes of the candidate, is probably the most important. Learning how they get paid, which products create commissions on any residual incomes, predicted monthly expenses, and so on, will give the candidate a general idea of how much work and how many sales are going to be required to generate a sufficient income for them and their family to live on.

Even if the candidate has told you what their past income was or what their expected income level should be, there will be a mysterious number that they need to feel comfortable that they can attain before they decide to make a career switch. You may never know what that income number truly is, but if you approach the compensation interview honestly and explain it completely, then if the candidate decides that with the compensation structure that you offer they can make an adequate income, then it is likely your candidate will join the organization.

Establishing a Licensing and Pre-contract Schedule

In those companies that require an insurance license prior to starting as an agent this meeting is a very important benchmark in the selection process. Often money has to be paid for the course materials and sometimes even an exam fee and whether that is borne by the recruiting company or the candidate, money has to be paid for the candidate has to go on with the selection process. Up to this point, it has been free of charge, educating conversations and a bit of business planning mixed in with dreaming. However, now someone has to pay to put this candidate on the path of working towards the required license to do business.

Licensing

If the candidate agrees to get into a study program with you, it is a good indication that all the other steps on the way have been understood and accepted by the candidate. That does not mean, however, that they don't need your help and guidance. Just because the candidate is willing to pay for textbooks does not mean they may not need to borrow your experience in setting a realistic schedule working towards a date or deadline to complete an exam. The manager has the best understanding of the depth and difficulty level of every chapter of the textbook. They will be able to set appropriate intervals for the candidate to come back in for threshold knowledge testing or additional tutoring on difficult chapters.

To adhere to what the candidate and the manager agreed to, working around the candidate's current work and vacation schedule of course, it is a good idea for both parties to agree and sign off on a timeline for a desired completion date. I generally recommend having a minimum of a once a week face-to-face meeting with the candidate to identify any trouble spots and to make sure they are completing the schedule as agreed.

It has been my experience that the duration of the study schedule is largely within the control of the candidate. I have seen people get through licensing requirements in three weeks and some people have taken it in three months. Regardless of however long it takes for a candidate to go through, I find it is a dangerous time for candidate because they switch from the excitement of a highly interactive interviewing process to one of a student often isolated at home reading a boring textbook on the dining table.

It is more important than ever during this phase of the selection process to remain connected to your candidate because as they learn the subject material they are constantly evaluating whether they see themselves in a career role that is using the products and concepts that are explained and they are judging whether or not they can do it. I would recommend a minimum of once a day contact with the candidate. This can take the form of a phone call, voice message, an email, a text message, or a tweet to let the person know that you're still thinking of them and believe that they can do this next step. Failure to do this is taking a big chance the candidate will lose enthusiasm during the long selection process many of our organizations have experienced. I have seen many candidates fade away during this time. It's a loss for them, and for us.

If you believe you have a high potential candidate in front of you but they are being hesitant to register for the study process, you can nudge them in gently or give them a comfortable way of backing out. Here is what I do; have the candidate pre-fill the registration form including credit card information then make an agreement that if they don't return the books in a week we will charge them for the price of the textbooks. However, if they return the book it won't cost them anything to read a few chapters and gain some insight into whether or not this career is suitable. If it isn't then we've both saved time, but if I'm right and they are really interested deep down, then we have not only progressed a few chapters into the licensing process but have also eased ourselves over a common stumbling block. More often than not, I find if people are given a test drive of a financial textbook and they do complete the first couple of chapters, they will contact you to let you know it's OK to process the payment. Very rarely do they return the textbooks, but deep down I feel that people who do hesitate appreciate the gesture that they are not locked into a decision.

Whether it is the manufacturer of the textbook or your company or your agency that develops quizzes that can be used for intervals during the study process, I find these as great opportunities to ensure that the candidate is not only reading the material but also comprehending the material. Simply highlighting and drawing in the textbook does not mean they understand the content ready for the exam format ahead. Oftentimes, exams have a fee associated with them so we do want our candidates to do everything possible to pass it on the first try. If possible, if you have additional resources such as flash cards, access to online videos, audio tracks or podcasts, or even old exams that you can give the candidate to sharpen their skills while going through the process, this can give you added insurance that your candidate will get through.

If you have a large number of candidates going through at the same time, it might be a good idea to do batch, or group, licensing training at your agency. Sometimes there are evening classes offered for a reasonable cost in your city that could assist students in passing the exams. The disadvantage of teaching in your agency is the time and coordination needed to make sure all the candidates are learning at the same pace, but the advantage is the training is provided for free. For outsourced training support, the advantage is it can be done on a self-paced basis and the disadvantage there is usually a substantial cost as well these can be hunting grounds for competitors to prospect for candidates who are already in the licensing process.

At the end of the tunnel there is the comprehensive threshold exam required for licensing. As this is the main event for all the weeks or months of interviewing, administration and studying, every effort should be made to give the candidate the best chance to pass. You can offer a prep class the week before, offer to arrange for pick up and drop off at the exam locations so they don't have to worry about traffic and parking so they can relax, and also offer something fun like taking the candidate out for a drink after the exam.

Once the exam is done, all you can do is wait for the result and depending on the situation it can take days or weeks to discover if the candidate has passed or not. Use this time to focus on the next step assuming that they are going to pass the exam. This is the opportunity to include them in branch training, social events, as well as work on distilling their market identification booklets to set up initial meetings or pre-contract sales to launch their first days as an agent. That way, if the results are positive, you've wasted no time getting that candidate productive in their new career. However, if the results come back negative, you have used that time to continue the education process and kept them engaged with your office versus sitting at home waiting for the results to come in.

Job Sampling and Pre-Contract Phase

Job sampling can be done throughout the selection process. It can include completing market identification booklets from 100-300 prospects that the candidate can connect to on a favorable basis. It can also incorporate needed paperwork such as market surveys, reference forms, and completion of financial needs analysis worksheets. The reasons to use job sampling is to show the client the job in an effort to screen out undesirable candidates, determine if there's a fit for your organization, and to identify any weak areas such as prospecting or asking for referrals. This is especially important when the candidate you are selecting comes from a non-sales career.

The focus of job sampling should be on the activity and enthusiasm of completion of tasks that are set for the candidate such as completing twenty market surveys by week's end. Using my background as a soldier as an example, obviously I had little experience with a sales environment or in initiating conversations for the purposes of business. I could not have formed an accurate picture of what the job entailed solely through the interview process or the contract licensing phase of selection. It was only through job sampling that I understood how difficult and exciting it was to meet with people to see if I could help. Some people will shine during this part of the selection process and other people will run away screaming.

Most large-scale and high-performing organizations use some level of pre-contract training and requirements to select their agents. Any sales count that needs to be satisfied should not be seen as another obstacle to be overcome by the candidate or recruiting manager but as another step of the selection process. It is their behaviour and performance during this final selection step that will tell you whether they are a long-shot candidate, a steady performer, or a shooting star. This is a good time to concurrently finish off any final administrative requirements for the head office as well as preparing the candidate for their first days at work as a new agent. It is imperative in the pre-contract phase to focus on their prospecting activity including personal observations and asking for referrals rather than simply sales activity.

Set a reasonable amount of time to complete their pre-contract requirements. In my experience anything more than four to six weeks may indicate cause for concern; however, in many circumstances we must remember that the candidate is also working at their current job while at the same time balancing personal obligations. If the candidate is unemployed then the pre-contract phase should be shortened because they have more time to focus. However, someone who is juggling family life alongside a 40 to 50 hour workweek may need some flexibility.

An extra note:

Around this time of the selection process, when both you and the candidate are getting more serious and even discussing timelines for contracting, they will ask for an appropriate time to notify their current employer of their impending career move. I usually tell them two things in this situation. First, there is no reason to tell their current boss because they are still weeks or months away from finishing their licensing process let alone the pre-contract period where they get to "job sample" the role before the jump in with both feet. This is a safe way to approach a career move, the way a good manager engenders trust is to never put their candidate in harm's way no matter how excited they or their candidate is to get on board. Remember to hire slowly, don't presume the outcome, and let the selection process do its job. There are many reasons you, or the candidate, may stop the process and at any time before contracting.

Second, once it is the right time to tell their current employer about their new career, I tell them what to expect. Often the reaction is positive and their supervisor understands that it's the best thing for the candidate to move forward despite losing a good employee. However, sometimes the reaction is not so positive. I give the candidate a professional heads-up that their employer may now offer them a raise or that promotion that's been long overdue in an effort not to lose them. I tell them to expect it, and if this situation happens, it forearms the candidate to not grab too fast at this offering. Why hadn't the employer offered the raise months ago? If they saw potential in their employee for advancement, why had they not make the decision *prior* to learning another organization also sees that potential and seized it?

The candidate should make the best decision for themselves and their families; whatever they decide we should respect. Every once in a while, after the above-mentioned scenario plays out the candidate returns to my office still full of conviction but are astounded that I predicted what their former boss offered. They are also proud that they had stood their ground in that moment.

The Law of 50 Percent

When attracting or training new managers, I find they often have a skewed understanding of how much work goes into contracting a new agent. They might believe they possess a superhuman skill of zoning in on a candidate then afterwards it's simply a matter of guiding them through the selection process. Voila, a new recruit is on board then let's go find another one! If only it was that easy!

When developing a plan with a new sales manager I try to blend this realistic formula with their idealistic expectations. This is also a good method when planning at an agency level the annual recruiting targets for your home office and you can work backwards through the formula to understand what activities to focus on to achieve the needed results. It has been my experience that a sales manager will typically lose half of their candidates in the selection funnel at every major step of the process. For example, to be realistic a recruiter or manager could think of their funnel this way:

Initial Contacts	50 candidates
Meet with you and agree to do pre-selection test	25
Pass aptitude 'test' and background check	12
Finish all interviews and register for licensing course	6
Complete course, obtain license and start pre-contract	3
Complete pre-contract and start with your agency	1

It is important as a sales manager to have a realistic expectation of the sheer volume of people that needs to be seen to yield a successful candidate that shows the capability and enthusiasm to join your organization. I find too often sales managers "fall in love" with their candidates and that they are sure that the hot prospect they are meeting with will certainly come on board to the agency. I've also seen sales managers that consider themselves snipers in that they will only be able to pick up the diamonds in the world around them that make good sales people in our industry and they won't bother talking to everybody else.

That being said, when I was a new sales manager I too had rose-coloured glasses on and I figured I had an instinctual radar for those people who had outstanding DNA as an agent. My mentor when I was a new sales manager coached me to assume that I would lose half of my candidates at every major step in the selection process. I was frustrated and a little dismayed about his words but after some years in the industry, I found he was absolutely right.

For example, if I talk to forty qualified prospects over the course of a month from networking events or my own personal observations, about half of them will agree to spend up to half an hour completing an aptitude test. And only half of those would yield a good enough result that I'm allowed to proceed with them. From there about half will register for the study process and pass the academic exam. And lastly, about half that start the job sampling and pre-contract stage will be offered a contract with our organization. Different candidate sources lead to different ratios.

Each candidate that drops offs doesn't mean they're "lost" forever; you can recycle many good candidates for consideration in future years. Create systems to keep in touch; we all get busy and you don't want to lose a great recruit amidst the "white noise" of running a business. One of my best agents, Gina Ramos won Regional Recruit of 2014 and has qualified for 2 conventions in a row. She was someone who looked at us, and we looked at her, for almost three years before eventually coming on board. Never give up; the great recruits are worth it.

Excellence With Humanity

Julie Cook

My father was the principal of a school in a small community in Southern Ontario and was responsible for creating the school motto.

Twenty-six years later when I found myself the new Branch Manager of an office that had no trust for management, no sense of identity or purpose, and lacklustre results, I felt it time to implement that school motto of my dad's—"Excellence with Humanity."

So what does that actually mean?

We hear people in business talking about "success" all the time but from what I hear people equate "success" with numbers: how much money they make, how big their house is, how their sales results compared to others.

To me the word we should be using instead is Excellence. Excellence is about setting a high standard for yourself and living to your full potential, whatever that is for YOU. Comparing yourself to others is an inaccurate and ineffective measurement. Instead, people who work to their own potential and strive to outperform their own bests achieve more and in a more satisfying way. Identify what your skills, abilities, hopes, and dreams are then apply the identified talents as best you can. Not everyone is created the same or has the same aspirations, so why do we compare ourselves to others? Why not work to your own potential?

> *"Do the best you can until you know better.*
> *Then, when you know better, do better."*
> **Maya Angelou**

The <u>Humanity</u> part is to remind us that we are part of a "we" as well as a "me." That in striving for excellence we must never step on someone to get where we want to be; that our words are truthful, our promises reliable, our actions respectful, our recommendations in the best interest of our clients. Without a significant purpose beyond pursuing society's common definitions of success, it's an empty accumulation of big screen TVs and massive square footage homes. When you look back over your career, you may wonder what it was all about.

Each individual will have their own purpose beyond the "me" and I believe the leadership of an agency needs to have a "we" mentality as well beyond the numbers, requirements, and rules of the office. Choose a charity, a community event, a cause that people can pull together toward and around. Doing something to change the world around you or even another person's life other than your own allows people to wake up each morning with a feeling of significance.

To begin implementation of this significant culture shift, I sat down with each advisor in my office and listened to them. Truly listened; practicing the use of two ears, one mouth. I kept my mind open, not thinking about what I'd say when it was my turn to speak. Get together outside the office without the trappings of spreadsheets and productivity charts; find out who the person is.

What gets them out of bed in the morning? Why did they join the insurance and investment world? Who is important to them? What are their hopes and thoughts for the future? When they give you the expected answers they are accustomed to giving such as "I want to qualify in the next sales campaign" or "I want to make a six-figure income this year" you should keep asking "Why?" Keep asking that until you get past the standard answers and into something of substance that tells you about the person you are sitting with and why that goal is important. This will only work if you are sincere in your listening efforts and desire to learn more. An advisor will sniff out a phony as quickly as you can spot a spray-on tan.

With a better understanding of the person and who that person is, I can then work alongside them to support them on their journey to Excellence. During my career I've repeatedly seen recruiting managers talking about how much money candidates could make or what travel reward they could earn without ever considering the person's motivations they are talking to. People are driven by so many different things: obtaining a CFP designation because they never went to university, rebuilding a professional career that was left behind when they immigrated to Canada, making enough income to own a home, being able to attend their child's school activities, or sending money back to their country of origin to put a younger sibling through school. The motivations are as varied as the people in your office.

If I know and understand their motivation, I can ensure my support is appropriately tied in. The single mom who wants to attend her children's school activities will not be motivated by yet another electronic device as a sales campaign incentive but she may be thrilled if your branch bought the shirts for the soccer team or the agency matches their contribution to that younger sibling back at their home country.

This attention to people's hopes and dreams creates an inspired, supportive atmosphere of advisors reaching for their best. This in turn increases the number of candidate referrals received to grow your agency because who wouldn't want to refer someone to a place where you are truly listened to, supported, and applauded! No longer were we attending career fairs and conducting exhaustive online resume searches as all our recruits came from agent referrals within.

And it's important to understand that as you go through this metamorphosis you will discover agents who are in the wrong seat on the bus you are driving, or maybe they shouldn't be on the bus at all. They could be a senior advisor who mentally got off the bus a long time ago but unfortunately still holds a seat or a new hire who should not have stepped on the bus in the first place. Take this as an opportunity to help them to another seat or move onto another bus. It is best for everyone in the long run.

Over the course of time, advisors understood we saw them as people, not numbers, and we wanted them to reach their own goals as much as they did. Our actions over time showed our words were truthful and we could be trusted. Our office was built of advisors proud of themselves, their colleagues, and the office they were part of.

"Thanks Dad."

By Julie Cook, FLMI, EPC
President of Upstage and 25-year career in management training, underwriting, field management, and a master recruiter
Mutual Life, Clarica, Sun Life Financial

Courage, Strength, Wisdom – Thoughts from a Life in the Field

Rob Popazzi

Since the early 1990s, I've known only one thing: the life insurance distribution system of the career agency model. Some would say that could limit one's perspective on things, others might suggest that it provides me with a unique perspective on the life of a sales manager. Without managers, the system simply does not exist. While the landscape has certainly shifted over the past two decades, there are some core themes that always seem to emerge when it comes to the success of managers and in turn the success of the system.

Courage

Not necessarily the run into a burning building sort of courage but the get up every day and dive into a world of constant leadership challenges kind. It may be a new market you are trying to expand your agency into, a new manager on your team that is struggling, a peer that is offside, or any one of a thousand other possible scenarios. As managers and leaders, you are presented these opportunities every day. It's about being courageous with your team, opening yourself up to the infinite possibilities that exist, and deciding on a path for yourself and your team. I've observed leaders fail as they've missed the moment that required courage.

If I can offer any advice, be aware of what's happening around you, plan for the future, and live in the present. When you are truly present, you will spot the opportunity and know that it is calling your name. Answer the call.

Strength

You need the strength to make the tough calls, to have the physical resilience and possessing the mental toughness to win. You need to be physically healthy as well as mentally strong. I've watched great leaders dedicate every waking minute to others only to find themselves broken and unable to keep up the pace. I've also lived it firsthand. I remember lying on my bed one day completely unable to get up due to a blown disc. It didn't happen overnight. It happened over 10 months of pouring myself into a new role and building a new team. We were getting results, but at what price?

Luckily, I was surrounded by great people that helped me grow and see the long game. I'm very aware of my physical well-being now and it helps me be mentally stronger as well. Strength is also about building the habits that will lead you to success. Managers and leaders understand how to grow an agency, how to develop people, and how to win business. By forming the habits that lead to these outcomes, day in and day out, you build strength of habit that can become unstoppable. You do the things that unsuccessful people are not willing to do, even when you don't want to do it yourself. That strength is key to winning.

Wisdom

This is really about having the wisdom to know when you don't know the answer. You know what you don't know and that helps you win. You also need to know who can be a mentor for you and who you need to develop for the next generation to be successful. You must understand "The Pygmalion Effect" in which our actions towards others impact others beliefs about us, which in turn will cause others actions towards us to change. This will reinforce our beliefs about ourselves, which influences our actions towards others. A self-fulfilling prophecy, if leveraged wisely, can transform a person, a team, or a culture.

I've watched amazing leaders take rookies, and with the wisdom of their experience and the passion of their convictions, help these people transform over time and grow into incredible leaders in their own right. For me the last component of wisdom is about developing the skill of learning. Are you helping your team develop their abilities to learn and grow? Are you working on your own? The continuous improvement mentality doesn't just apply to manufacturing shops any more. We all need to be working on ourselves, looking for those small wins that will add up to major success.

Any one of these three attributes by itself won't make for a great manager or leader. You need to see all three working in harmony to really win. There are many other components to your roles and they all play a part. As a leader, you have signed up for a different career path. One that I feel is truly noble. I think it's important to note that for me, regardless of your distribution model or even industry, these core attributes have to be present for all of your other skills and talents to be really leveraged.

Leaders serve and sacrifice. That's what makes them leaders. In our model, we change people's lives. This isn't pretend. People join our industry expecting to win. They've bought into our vision and our system and most importantly, they've bought into the leader. Let's do everything we can to ensure their career path is a long and successful one.

If you are reading this, you are a leader looking to grow or you may be just embarking on your leadership journey. Either way, please dive into the many ideas that are in this book, think about how you can weave a few of them into how you live, and work and start thinking about the legacy you will leave behind. The future generations of clients, beneficiaries, businesses, and advisors need you to take this seriously.

We are one group of leaders on a continuum of time that stretches back hundreds, if not thousands, of years and will stretch forward for an even longer period of time. We will not be here to really see the impact of our actions. With a purpose, a vision, and the courage, strength, and wisdom to drive ourselves forward every day, I am confident the future will be incredible.

By Rob Popazzi, BA, CLU, CHS
AVP Sales Force Growth and Development
Sun Life Financial

Points to Remember from this Section

1. Know how other industries pay commissions
2. Law of 50 Percent
3. Expand your recruiting market opportunities

Now add points you want to remember or refer back to:

-
-
-
-

Notes:

_____

_____

_____

_____

_____

_____

Section 3

Developing Agents and Managers

Training and Development

It's one thing to get people on board with your agency; it's another to build their needed skills and habits to be productive. Joint fieldwork is often a means to an end in the pre-contract phase, but I find there is a direct correlation between the success of an agent and the amount of joint fieldwork done after contracting. Remember we are selling a client-resistant, intangible product. After selling an insurance product or setting up a new investment account, there isn't much to show the client. Even if they really understand the need for putting the coverage in place, there isn't the same satisfaction in buying something more sexy and tangible like say a new iPhone. Train on the ways to create something for the client to "see and hold."

For example, for a $225 per month investment show that at a 5 percent rate of return after 35 years it will yield $250,000. Show them this and remind them of what they're building towards at every annual review. Also, communicate to them often about what happens if they start raising their contribution in a couple of year by $10 per month over that timeframe. Now it's almost $400,000 more; that shows the value of your professional advice and service, and that's more exciting than an iPhone!

Stress the importance of not getting confined early into one favoured product line. We have all had "termite" agents that only sell term products to their market. Sometimes these agents are nervous about asking for larger premiums associated with health and permanent life sales. Other times it's because they are fast and easy sales; the clients don't offer many objections for a $30 per month premium. This can occur naturally when someone is learning how to sell our products, but I've also seen well-meaning senior agents giving rookies ideas for quicker sales, not always understanding that this can put them on a path that leads to below-average incomes.

Stop this tendency before it begins with your agents or step in to mitigate it right away. Cross train diverse product lines early in the training process, expose them to ideas that include starting with term to convert some to permanent within one year, and how to retain medically declined cases with guaranteed-issue products. You can also coordinate experienced agents to help demonstrate how to conduct proper needs analyses with prospects and how to comfortably ask for higher premiums.

Another way to develop good agents is help them develop "Step 2" in their sales process when working with clients. Most agents out there, especially the part-time ones, are only trained in "Step 1" sale concepts that begin and end when a solution is provided. Any professional that can explain that they have a Step 2 for a client will show more value than a single step sales concept. For example, a client is interested in a critical illness product in case they have cancer or a heart attack during their prime career or child-rearing years. The agent sells them an adequate critical illness insurance product. Now the client is happy to have the protection and the agent is happy for the commission and a new client.

However, the story doesn't have to end there, at least not for an agent that has a Step 2. The agent can put a "return of premium on cancellation" rider on the critical illness insurance that will return all premiums paid to the client when they cancel the insurance at age 65. Here's where step two comes in: take all that returned premium and put it into a life annuity. It has been my experience that the monthly premiums they have paid into the insurance product can be doubled as an amount paid to the client as an endless retirement income. This is a Step 2 concept that will impress the client, gain loyalty, and certainly make them more "sticky" when competing agents speak to them over the years and will likely make the agent more referable in a competitive marketplace. Creating a Step 2 plan can be achieved with virtually any product or service our agents sell.

Organization is key to any business to ensure their agents document details of conversations, needs analyses, follow-up expectations, and so on. Additionally, it's important not to lose track of potential business, and this can happen accidentally. By creating systems, you can eliminate problems like this. For example, in February a client says they're too busy now but want you to follow up six months later in August. You put a reminder in your digital calendar on your smartphone or laptop and move onto your next task.

Another way to handle this situation is to have a twelve-month louvered filing system that can be attached to the wall beside your desk or your assistant's desk. Each slot is marked in descending order from January to December. Now all you have to do is make a note detailing what needs to be done in six months or you could even put the prospect's entire file into the slot marked "August." When that month comes around simply pull out the note and resume the process with the prospect. Make systems for organizing and dealing with repetitive tasks and you'll solve the problems. This can make your assistant's life a lot easier and if you don't have one then when you do, it's easier to learn how you do things and leverage their administrative skills that much faster.

Rookie Training (six months in the business)

At the risk of being personally attacked on this topic, I like to train my advisors at a 12-year-old's level of comprehension and ask them to educate clients at the same comprehension level. This is not to say that advisors are children or that clients have below average intelligence but it's the level needed for a financial concept to be understood more easily and accurately be passed on to another person. For example, an agent could explain to a client how a life annuity works using such things as indexing mortality credits, guaranteed periods, and so on. This may lose the client's interest and understanding. However, if the agent explains to a client that essentially an annuity is like a bucket that somebody puts a large dollar amount into then later they can punch a hole in the bottom of the bucket to drip out income steadily for the rest of their life. That, most people can understand and may be able to tell a neighbour how annuities work.

I find that being able to teach and reinforce basic principles of finance and, more importantly, to make these concepts "sticky," it has to be done at a level that is easy to understand, apply, and transfer to another person. The reason why this is important is that oftentimes when we are in front of clients they are not the sole decision-makers and will often have to wait and discuss with a business partner, spouse, trusted uncle, etc. before moving ahead. For them to accurately relay information regarding a product or financial concept reliably to that second person requires that the concept be summarized and illustrated in a way that a 12-year-old would understand. Somebody could explain that concept mentioned above versus a twenty-page illustration on expectations, definitions and assumptions.

Basic essentials of training new agents revolve around the must-know features of the early parts of a rookie's business such as compliance, application process, prospecting, closing, business planning, needs analysis, ordering paramedical visits, and such. I believe basic product information should be limited to a handful of products such as term, permanent life, critical illness, and health and dental. It is impossible to teach every feature benefit of every product line in the first several months; don't even try to do it. Not only does this take too much time, but we do not know if the agent's business plan encompasses every product. Furthermore, we do not want to turn a new, eager, commission-driven agent into boardroom student.

It has been my experience that is better to have multiple training opportunities over a week versus having an in-house training day boot camp. This all-in-a-day concept is like locking someone in a classroom for a 10-hour day then expecting them to play at the same level if they had 5 lessons at 2 hours each over a week. Common sense would say that the latter teaching structure would yield better results. There is only so much the brain can take in and apply. It needs opportunities to work with learned concepts whether successful or not and then come back to the training.

If possible, have the rookie come in two to three times a week for half days, give them not only educational homework and expectations but also sales activity and expectations in the same week. I believe that strong advisors not only need to be able to work but they also need to be able to continue learning while working. Never more than now has this challenge been a reality; the continual learning while working a business practise is only going to get more fast-paced in the future with compliance changes, insurance products changing every 3-5 years, tax structures updating annually, investment markets change daily. The only constant in an advisor's world is change. What they knew a year ago may not be sufficient next year.

For the rookie training session I believe it is beneficial to break it down to three components being administrative, technical, and sales-oriented. For example, on a training day that covers term insurance, the administrative piece would show how the term insurance product works in the application process and what purposes it serves for the marketplace. The technical piece would be how to illustrate and prepare quotes for clients using software or forms, and the sales piece would be on how to actually approach and position term products for prospects including the common objections often heard with that product.

A fun way to verify the rookie's understanding of products throughout the training period is the High 5 technique. For example, at the end of teaching a session on term life, I would say give me five reasons why term life is a good product for young couples. Around the room, answers will start flying such as: high death benefit, low cost, convertibility, renewable and cancellable, beneficiaries get benefit tax-free, and so on. What this exercise will have done is drive in key features and how to relate key information to clients to make a decision. Even if agents don't remember all five points, they might remember three or four when the time is right.

This technique can be used for any insurance product or investment vehicle and can be applied even to specific markets. For just-in-time training it can be used to sharpen the recall and comprehension of the new advisors on the spot. I have sometimes stopped a rookie I met down the hallway and said "Hey Jack, give me five reasons why someone should look at critical illness insurance" and stood there while they give me the five reasons. This can be fun, spontaneous, and even generate an unforeseen conversation regarding a potential sales opportunity with a client that evening.

Some common "High 5" subjects that I enjoy when training rookies are:

- 5 Benefits of a critical illness insurance
- 5 Strengths of permanent life insurance
- 5 Reasons for buy-sell arrangements
- 5 Benefits of RESPs

- 5 Advantages of mutual funds
- 5 Responses to an objection

Many companies have head office developed and driven training programs and binders. I believe that these are valuable and are the best way for a new sales manager to get acquainted with the training philosophy and to be able to show value quickly in an advisor's career. However, I believe these developed training programs are a beginning of new agent education and not the end. I often make the analogy that the binders we use in the first six months of a new advisors' development provide the black and white of what we're trying to accomplish but it is the experience and the enthusiasm of the sales manager to bring color into the training within that black and white environment. A great way to do that and to add credibility to your in-house training program is to augment these basic training points with advice from successful advisors in your agency.

For example, when speaking to rookies about working in the family market, as well as the products and sales concepts they are attracted to, have an experienced advisor assist in these conversations. You can also use these established agents in training events discuss how they leverage your compensation system and resources to qualify for convention. If those advisors are pre-briefed by the sales manager on the training group's understanding as well as what messages you would like to deliver about the subjects on that day, the rookie advisor will get the most out of the opportunity to learn from the older advisors. Oftentimes, I get better attendance not only from my rookie advisors but also from those advisors who have graduated (they go back to class when they hear seasoned advisors are attending the training).

At the end of rookie training, the graduation from the rookie school should be marked as an accomplishment. How grand the graduation process is up to you; it can range from invite the advisor and their spouse for an evening out and present a certificate either by yourself or with their mentor, or as simple as having lunch with the agent to celebrate this significant milestone. As a reward for successfully passing the rookie training, you can offer an opportunity to move to the next level in their business development. Paying for an additional license, awarding gift certificates for a designation course, or giving them a small block of business are ways of doing that.

Advanced Classes (six months to two years)

The advanced classes should immediately start when the rookie classes have ended. Whereas the rookie classes are mandatory, there are benefits to these more "optional" classes that are open to any advisors who are under two years in the business. Once in a while I would restrict admission to the advance classes to those who have performed to a specific production level the previous month or who had qualified in the last sales campaign. The challenge to the sales manager is to provide concrete sales concepts that yield results. Unfortunately, sometimes struggling advisors will attend advance classes because it's something to do that day. Their presence in the classes can weaken the others that are functioning at a higher level.

I think it is important to vary the feel and content of these classes compared to the rookie sessions. Assume that all basic information has been learned from the previous rookie classes and now it is time to leverage that base knowledge. It is like children starting grade 4, the teacher will not review the alphabet with the class; they properly assume they already have this foundation to be able learn move further in the curriculum. For an agent, this progressive structure is where more complex concepts and applications of familiar products can stretch an advisor's thinking to provide creativity and ideas of how to approach different markets.

Once in a while, where appropriate, have these training sessions out of the agency and somewhere that is connected to your topic. For example, if you are going to teach "long-term care product concepts" arrange a field trip to your local retirement home with one of your top long-term care advisors to help do the training there. After the rookies have learned about the product and how it fits, they can tour the facility and meet the seniors who live there to hear real stories and learn about the cost and environment of the facility.

Make training real and this will ensure that your advisors never forget your training.

Also, as with advance training in our childhood years, I find it beneficial to keep advisors accountable to homework and some of their own development. The trainer can give them a concept, reading materials, and have them solve a case study to present to their peers in the next session. This will allow everyone to learn and apply new concepts. The sales manager at this point can take less of a teaching role and more of a facilitative role where they can develop the content of agenda of the training but a lot of their time will be in sourcing expertise and finding new ways to teach advisors.

There is a limitless supply of third-party presenters in our industry. If you are speaking about wealth products, have a mutual fund company present. If you are talking of RESP, talk to a university program director, or if government benefits, have a CPP consultant speaker to that session. Anything that can be done to provide a diverse outlook on different product types will provide another angle for advisors to pick up something new.

Whereas the rookie class is several times a week, the advance class should be weekly or even fortnightly. Hopefully the advisors have learned to be active and how to survive in business. Similar to the rookie class, a marked occasion for graduating the advanced class should be observed (but raise the stakes a little). You can coordinate graduation ceremonies with a visiting vice president to assist you in presenting a graduation speech and giving out certificates. The agency can offer special recognition to the "top of the class" that year and that can be fun and inspire agents to apply themselves. A professional gesture like a signed book by the president of the company or a dinner out with a VP can make an impact.

Advisor University

We have called this training advisor group several things in the past such as the "premium club" or "convention club" to keep it fresh but at the end of the day, it's a forum to discuss advanced concepts as well as sharing the best practises in every aspect of a financial advisor's business. One day it could be how to build a 10 million dollar wealth book of business while another session can speak on strategies of succession planning in retirement years, and so on.

I believe in an "admission ticket" philosophy and so everyone who attends this session should have earned their seat. You can make up whatever criteria you wish. I heard some managers keep it to ten or more years in the business to attend or the agent has qualified for MDRT or convention. I do find that the more prestigious you make the group, the more they want to attend it. Invite only successful agents, don't 'dilute' the peer quality they will be sharing their ideas with. I suggest that senior managers facilitate these sessions, not the junior sales managers. It should be done monthly or quarterly, because in every session there should be a value for the senior advisors to come.

For those motivated by personal development, create an education system or even an "agency university" that offers training or focus groups that keep progressing as their skills and business models change.

Be an Expert at Compensation and Income Streams

One of the most important components of any career is how a person is compensated for they work they do. This is no different for people in our industry. Compensation can also be important from a client point of view as it can drive the behaviour of the agent to some degree. If you look at the agent's contract, are they paid to place business or to maintain it, or a bit of both? The longer you work in the career the more income you can make because as your block size increases so should your ability to generate income from it. In terms of sales of product types, that too can influence behaviour. If an agent gets paid more commission on life insurance sales than they do on disability insurance that can drive behaviour too if the agent can accumulate significant residual incomes for a large block which can stimulate behaviour linked to long-term income planning.

Understanding Level versus Heaped Compensation Models

How does the agent's compensation affect the client? If the agent gets compensated more for placing the business, which is common in heaped commission models, I have seen it affect long-term service levels in the client's experience. For example, a real estate agent get large lump sum commissions for completing a transaction once the buyer get the key to their new home. Beyond a welcome gift basket being dropped off, there isn't much thinking about on the agent's part about what happens afterwards. The real estate agent is not motivated or incented to follow up or have annual meetings with the homebuyers because they have made their money from the transaction and the clients are not likely to purchase another home in the short term. Onto the next client looking for another lump sum commission they go and they can never get off the hamster-wheel. Even if they have 17 years of happy clients put into beautiful homes behind them, if they want to make income next month they better sell a home next month.

In contrast, on a levelized commission system there are significant commissions paid at the time of the transaction but also ongoing renewal commission that compensates the agent periodically for retaining the client long term. Clients benefit from this arrangement because agents are motivated to provide ongoing service for the long term as well. Even if the business was placed nine years ago, the agent is still earning commission for keeping the client happy. If the client wants a policy review or change in their beneficiaries, that agent will call that client back quickly.

For example, a client does a $100 monthly premium insurance sale ($1,200 annual premium paid over 12 months). In a heaped system, brokerage world they often pay 120 percent annually, equalling about $1,500 commission for that agent. In contrast, an advisor working for a levelized commission system can make about 100 percent of the annual premium, about $1,200. However, they also could make about $5-$10 a month of "service" commission for retaining that client's business. An agent-client relationship that is based on a transactional commission is more likely to generate a client only seeking out an agent to change policy or when they ask for servicing. The agent, unless they feel a new piece of business is possible often isn't motivated to spend much time on servicing on a transactions that occurred 7, 10 or 20 years ago. In contrast, the agent-client relationship based on a levelized transaction will motivate the behaviour from an agent point of view, the longer the client stays with the agent by month or by year or by decade, the more income is generated.

It's not to say that an agent on a levelized commission structure does a better job that a heaped commission agent but many behavioural psychologists would say the latter might motivate different agent-client relationships. The heaped relationship, like a real estate agent, can never get off the commission hamster wheel. Even if that realtor has been in business for 12 years, on a heaped commission system if they want to make an income next month they have to sell a house next month as they don't receive on-going commissions on their past clients. On a levelized system, the agent is building ongoing, stable residual income based on those 12 years of keeping the client. I would wager that if an agent knew their long-term income depended on educating, placing, and supporting financial sales they would pay attention to it more.

Agents in levelized models are motivated to service their clients literally, and figuratively, to death.

Income Diversification – Choosing an Elevator

As with any business, there are benefits to having multiple income streams from diversified product lines. So understanding the commission structure for each of those product lines is important. The commission structure for individual life and health products, group benefits, investments, annuities, and so on all pay the agent differently. I believe a well-rounded business practise should incorporate all these lines where possible. This is also important for agents who want to receive more stable commissions throughout the year. We all know sales of some product lines are seasonal; in autumn our industry sells more insurance products and in summer we sell more group and investment products. Product sales can also be affected by economic cycles. In times of boom, economic clients tend to want to pay attention more on investment products. In times of economic downturns, people and companies tend to move toward protection products and value group benefits more.

For example, after the panic of 2008 people's investment portfolios shrunk by 30 to 40 percent. However, for the two years that followed many insurance companies experienced greatly increased sales. Families and individuals were buying insurances to protect their incomes, to pay their mortgages if something unfortunate happened, and to get rapid treatment to get back on their feet if they were critically ill. Further, we also saw small to medium-sized companies increase or augment their group benefits for their employees in efforts to both retain good workers but also to attract good talent from struggling companies nearby who had to let workers go.

From 2012 to present as economies, employment rates, and housing sales improve, we find many people are now returning in higher numbers for investment conversations. The financial industry is very fortunate; we can swing our guns to target what clients and businesses want. In times of trouble, we swing to large amounts of affordable protection like term and guaranteed investment products, but in good times, we swing more to participating whole life sales and market-based investment. Unlike the vast majority of industries out there, we are recession-proof.

I love pictures and analogies to make points, especially tongue-in-cheek ones! Here is a question to pose to your agents while training them on building a holistic business: if there were another financial earthquake, which elevator would YOU want your business practise to be in? The one on the left represents a single income stream like those seen by agents who sell one product line (e.g. like "term-ite" agents who only sell term life products). The elevator on the right one represents a practise with several cables showing multiple income streams. These advisors work with investments, group benefits, health insurance, estate planning, life insurances, and so forth. Any rookie can understand these simple images in training class and it's often an "aha" moment on the importance of diversifying their income sources.

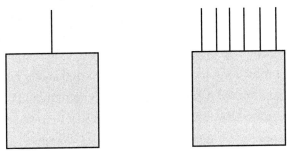

Part-time and Full-time Advisor Incomes

The regulatory environment in many countries, including Canada, allows for a part-time financial agent. A person can choose to be a part-time agent for many reasons: to augment their regular income, they may be unable to work full-time (like a stay home mom), or someone may want to "try out" financial services before committing. I may not be popular saying it but, generally speaking, these part-timers detract from the professionalism, dedication, appropriate product placement, and service levels that should be provided to the client. Whereas the government regulators are comfortable with having part-time agents in the financial arena, I personally would be dubious as a client working with someone that only took care of my financial needs part-time while working in a coffee shop. A funny thought to ponder; would YOU want a part-time doctor to treat you who also works at a restaurant? I thought not. When it comes to medical and financial matters I would want a full-time professional where this is all they do for a living. I apologize for my rant. From this point on, we will talk about working with and training the full-time advisor.

For financial agents, what kind of incomes can they expect? The average income in my city in 2012 was about $45,000 a year, as taken by a government census, and for a dual-income household was about $63,000. An advisor with a reputable company, adequate training, and a well-rounded product line should expect a good comparative income in the initial years. For example, it has been my experience that first-year agents earn $50,000 to $60,000 in their first full year. By the end of the third full year, it should be $90,000 to $100,000 from all income sources. Most people would say that's pretty good!

During the initial stages of talking to a candidate, they will start to dream and get excited about unlimited incomes. They will invariably ask, "Can I make $100,000 in my first year?" To this question I usually answer, "Yes of course you can; however, only the top 20 percent accomplish this. So together, let's build a business plan that can get you this income then afterwards you can tell me if you're willing to work hard to make that plan a reality."

Everyone knows in any sales environment the most difficult years to survive are the first three. If an advisor makes it to the third year, they should have an adequate income from the diverse sources of the product lines they sell. Some incomes pay monthly like investment trailers and some pay annually like group benefit renewals and insurance. By this time, they have established a base of clients they can service, cross-sell, and obtain prospect referrals from. With all these advantages combined, they will receive adequate income and likely jeopardize it by leaving the business.

Ratios of compensation by product line will change over the years for an agent. It has been my experience when it comes to income source that in the first five years it tends to be 75 percent from insurance sales and 25 percent from all other sources such as investment commissions and trailers and group benefits. However, in the following five to ten years in the business agents tends to have a 50/50 split, half from insurance sales and half wealth and group. After ten years in the business, the weighting flips to the majority of an agent's income coming from investment products and group with the smaller portion coming from commissions from individual insurance sales. The above scenarios are based on average production levels of $50,000 annual insurance premiums each year with $3 million of new wealth business done per year.

The common concern for a rookie agent is if they can make enough income to be able to survive the initial years and have a good long-term income. From a client's point of view, the concern is often if the agent is getting paid too much commission and this can lead to distrust that the agent is not suggesting appropriate solutions. (Note: to relieve a client's concern, the government and industry regulators will not allow us to be paid out of proportion for the services that we provide). If an agent comes into this career and works hard for the first three years, they would make good sustainable income. Work exceptionally hard and they will get an exceptional income, it's simple math.

Medical doctors make good money because their practise is built over many years in their community. I personally know both medical specialists and financial advisors making great incomes but it took them decades to build a practise to earn that. Conversely, if you want to make money fast then this is not the industry to do it, but for anyone looking for a sustainable above-average income and a comfortable lifestyle, you can't get much better than this. Persevere and it will pay off.

When recruiting and training new advisors on how they get paid, it's important to give them real life examples that they will experience in the market. If they have a specific ethnic market, for example, ensure you give them realistic income expectations as well as suggest the product lines that market will likely gravitate towards. Certain markets like term insurance because of affordability, other markets see term as an expense or a waste of money so they gravitate to permanent life insurance products that have high cash values. Term insurance as a general rule pays less than permanent insurance, and this is true not only because of the lower premiums paid by the client but the manufacturers place a commission emphasis on permanent products as these tend to be "sticky" business. Therefore, if an agent works in a market that is predominantly attracted to term, or permanent, you need to adjust how you set their income expectations.

Keep in mind that during recruiting and initial training they are taking in an incredible amount of information. If you explain at a 12-year-old level, they will better retain and communicate it well with their partner. It is critical in the initial stages that they can comprehend and articulate one of the most important parts of this industry. This very true at the recruiting stage: are they able to discuss it with their spouse over dinner versus some highly complex compensation structure that only someone from NASA would understand? If the how they get paid is too complicated it creates doubt and virtually no one will make a career change based on something they don't fully understand. They will earn a living from a sales career where there are big fluctuations in commissions. They probably won't complain to you if they get paid too much but they will knock on our door if they think they got paid too little this month.

It is an unfortunate aspect of human psychology that some apologize for success. Why is this? It has been my experience that people grow up or surrounded by peers of a certain socio-economic range. If people are raised in a household gaining $50,000 a year for example, then their perception of what is a comfortable or familiar lifestyle will be based on that income range. I find also that people have a certain "income buffer" of about 10-20 percent in either direction before they become a bit uncomfortable. So in our example above, an agent raised in a household that earned $50,000 annually may be comfortable somewhere between $40, 000 to $60,000. To get them thinking out of this range will sometimes take coaching.

Create a More Predictable Income for your Agents

Setting up an advisor's new income expectation is a matter of planning, and so is budgeting it. Income can be a source of stress at home, especially the fluctuating commission incomes that they experience. Find out what is the agent's required income and desired income. For example, because of financial obligations or current lifestyle, the agent needs to make $4,000 per month but they desire $6,000 a month income. They have the goal, now they have to plan to make it happen.

A technique to work around the peaks and valleys of our commission world is to set up two separate bank accounts. The first account is where the agent's gross commissions from sales are deposited. As we all know, commissions can be affected by seasonality, sales campaigns, landing large cases, changing closing ratios, and underwriting declines so we cannot always control, or predict, an agent's monthly income. However, by directing the gross income into the first account we can set up systematic auto-transfers of specified amounts to the second account. This second account is where the agent's family can make budgets and pay their household expenses from.

For example, when the agent makes a commission income of $7,000 in their first month it will go to the first account. They have set an automatic transfer to the second account of $4,000 that will satisfy their family's monthly budget. For the second month, the agent earns only $3,000 commissions but this is now added to the $3,000 remaining in the first account so they are still able to make the $4,000 transfer to buy groceries and pay the mortgage. There is still $2,000 in the first account to be used to "smooth" future incomes and the agents can let the first account "hold" the surplus indefinitely or ideally it can be paid as a year-end "bonus" to themselves.

If the agent starts making consistently better commissions then perhaps move their systematic transfers from $4,000 to $5,000 per month. This artificial "stabilizing" of commission income will give the spouse some comfort and allow them to plan without additional stress. Months of high and low commissions can be stabilized through this two-account system. The agent may not want to keep it forever but I've seen this technique save new agents in the initial years.

Creating a Monthly Agency Newsletter

Having a monthly in-house newsletter is a great way to communicate to large groups. Much of its construction and data-entry can be done by administrative staff at your agency. It might only take about two hours to make your own version using the monthly newsletter template provided. An added bonus is where these agency flyers end up; one time a spouse called asking how far her spouse was to qualify for convention in Hawaii, and another time an outside agent saw our CFP designation classes offered and asked to join our group. Additionally we know they read it. How do we know this? Easy, the agents call and protest when there is a small error in their numbers or we missed something they wanted to brag about!

Distribute these monthly "brag sheets" at least monthly, it's easy to skip getting these done when the agency is extremely busy. Print on coloured sheets of paper to put in their mailbox and send out digitally in pdf formats to make it mobile. Put as many faces as you can in each edition and find a reason to promote everyone at least once a year, even if it's their birthday.

Some components that I've seen work on this one-page, double-sided coloured paper are shown below. Feel free to use this template in its entirety or as a foil to brainstorm your own monthly flyer. Use as much imagery and advisor faces as you can pack into it. For really big accomplishments have a picture of the agent with their spouse.

FRONT PAGE

1. Annual convention destination, dates, and qualifying criteria
2. Top junior agent for insurance, show total annual premium
3. Top junior agent for wealth, show total deposits for the month
4. Top senior agent for insurance
5. Top senior agent for wealth
6. Agency training schedule for the current month with topics, speaker names, and holidays agency is closed
7. Next branch meeting announcement, date, and guest speakers

8. Next month's social event details
9. Top 10 health sales agents, and show the next two who are close
10. "Premium Club" – Top annual premium, list agents in descending order, over $5,000 annual premium
11. Agents tracking MDRT and rookies in mentor program, upcoming conference details

BACK PAGE

12. Agents tracking for convention qualification and what they need to make it
13. Sales campaign trackers, either head office of agency created
14. New recruits contracted, photos and names
15. Significant anniversaries, retirements, and designations earned last month

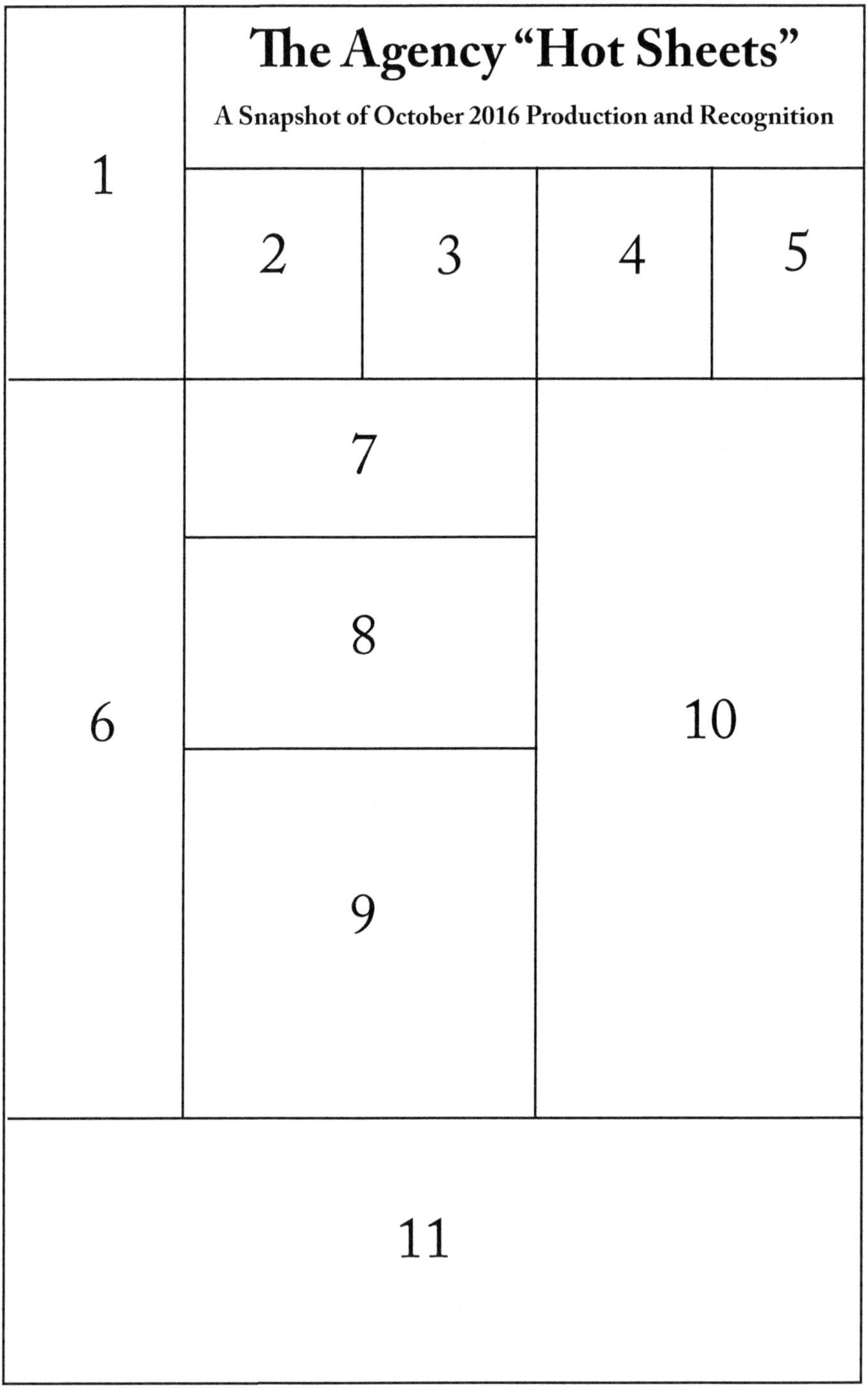

1

The Agency "Hot Sheets"

A Snapshot of October 2016 Production and Recognition

2 **3** **4** **5**

6

7

8

9

10

11

Convention Trackers

12

Sales Campaign Update

13

Welcome Aboard!

14

Special Announcements

15

Mid-Year Performance Letter – Example

A great way to communicate to your above-average agents is with a "report card" that illustrates the items and accomplishments that matter to them, not the agency. A typical time to do this is at the beginning or end of the calendar year but you can also distribute these personalized letters in the summer time. It creates an opportunity to see them near the middle of the year to not only show them where they have gone already in the year but how they can affect the outcome of the year with the time they have left!

If you have a larger agency, you may not be able to make letters for everyone so you can be selective. I have used this format for "bronze" agents and above, which is based on several criterions I think are good for a well-rounded agent but you can make your own parameters. Creating the actual letters doesn't have to be time intensive; your assistant can make a spreadsheet that covers all the points then you can mail merge the fields. Make sure you print it on your business letterhead and put your signature on it; these touches count! Someone should read the letter before it is mailed to their home address (remember the spouse will read it too) and I always try to put something personal as a note on the bottom.

Congratulations (Agent name), you are halfway through 2016 and looking great!

Time goes by so fast; it seems like we just had our AGM! You have been with us for almost two years, wow! You just came back from Convention and have had a great start to the year. Good luck at making this your best year ever!

You have made some amazing accomplishments in recent months. The most recent was **qualifying in Spring Campaign**. I'm proud to say your business is growing:

- **Your retirement package,** as of May 2016's statement, is already $1,680 a month payable for the next 10 years!
- You are on track for over **$135,000** income in 2016 with our agency! That's in the top 4 percent of income earners in North America; imagine what you will achieve in the next five years.
- You are one of the most **health active** advisors we have with **36 sales** of Disability, Critical Illness, or Long term Care insurance!
- Your insurance **"trailer" commissions** are over $1,900 per month.
- Your **wealth trailer income** from your $15 million AUM is almost $2,300 per month and your goal was $2,500. I think you can close the gap in the next few months.
- You are on track to earn the prestigious **Diamond Level,** and could earn your **Production Ring** this year! You are on track for writing more than 100 cases this year!
- You could qualify for your first MDRT conference and I'm looking forward to spending some time with you in Los Angeles next year.

Going forward I know you have several goals before next year's Gala Event that will recognize accomplishments in 2016which could include:

- Qualifying in **Summer and Fall Campaign** for a clean sweep of sales campaigns
- Qualifying **Convention in Dominican Republic** for you and your wife Beth

You have become one of our best financial advisors and it's a pleasure to have in our agency. A fantastic 2016 is within your grasp!

Be great!
Greg Powell

Marketing for Managers – Get your Message out There

A very intelligent lady and a great recruiter in the industry shared her mantra with me: Does everyone in the community know you are hiring? Does everyone know why they should work with you? Does everyone on your team know the branch's goals and mission in the community? This is a big part of my marketing philosophy as someone whose emphasis includes finding and selecting talent for our agency.

Great marketing can have similar properties to a new organism being formed. Cells share their "code" by dividing and multiplying at a logarithmic rate. In an ideal world, your message will take on a life of its own. Share your "agency code" with your managers, agents, centres of influence, and community networks.

Being an ex-army guy, I like keeping things simple. We can break the process down into common-sense steps that will always be there for you when you need them.

Step 1: What is the message you want to send out?

Be bold, be brief, and be done! Your message could be about an opportunity for a new agent, staff, or manager position this year. It does not always have to be about recruiting either. Perhaps you are creating a satellite office or have a position for a succession plan that you need assistance filling. Your agency might even be holding a large community event that can accommodate 10,000 attendees. Remember, any marketing message has to be "sticky" to stay in the minds of others after you are no longer with them. You want to leave a person with an impression or a thought that they keep rolling over in their mind that day. Once you have created your powerful message then you will have a passion to begin spreading the word. Sooner or later though, you'll find yourself realizing a natural limitation: you are only one person and there are lots of people out there.

Step 2: A team to carry the message.

The challenge mentioned above can be overcome by enlisting the help of others. This can be daunting but don't be lured into the trap of doing this alone as it will greatly reduce your chances of success. The adage of many hands make light work is absolutely true. Remember: others are juggling workloads and personal lives so you need to make carrying the marketing message convenient, fun (if possible), and address the "what's in it for me" factor.

Convenience is a key element to attracting assistance. Routinely give advisors material or small marketing items to include in letters to clients or to give out during meetings. Create a one-page sheet with your message and make it easy to read and containing photos of people in your agency or a recent fun branch activity. By the way, if the advisors agree to mail your message to their block of business offer to offset their mailing costs by paying for stamps, stationary, etc.

Ask one of your team leaders to create a campaign especially for distributing an agency message. You could have an in-house competition for the best cost-effective idea to distribute and then a second competition to name a winner for the most successful idea (judged by number of messages delivered to people). Cash, seasonal prizes, or cool experiences such as ballooning or white-water rafting can generate interest.

Step 3: Find opportunities for the message to "get out" there.

Once you have the message and have methods of impacting large amounts of people, the next step is to arrange opportunities to get in front of your "target markets" in your community.

Mail the agency newsletters (you may want to do some editing) or your newly created one-page sheet to your Centres of Influence and the agency's peripheral professionals (e.g. lawyers, notaries, funeral homes, and fee-for-service nursing) to make available at their places of business.

Annual community festivals and tradeshows, semi-annual convocations at local post-secondary institutions, and ongoing charity events are great places to start building your calendar. Pre-loading this schedule at the beginning of the year allows you to designate team champions to take ownership of events and allocate your marketing dollars effectively.

You can also make your own opportunities by offering public presentations or donating your time with "Life 101" seminars for new BBA or MBA graduates. If you really want to try something unique then find a local college or university that is willing to help you organize a reversed trade show. This is where the students (or similar targeted group, of course) create booths marketing their strengths to you and other would-be employers that you invited that evening.

At all these occasions, you can easily provide your agency message and follow up with a coffee next week to discuss.

Be infectious, share your code to as many carriers as you can.

Succession Planning – A Storm is Coming

In my previous career as a soldier I learned a couple of things that translate well in my current career as a financial sales manager in the 21st century. The attack will happen on two occasions: a) when you're ready, and b) when you're not.

In the military, we create succession plans upon receiving a position of leadership. Within days of shaking out your team and understanding individual strengths and weaknesses, you had to decide an order of replacement. The reality was that if you were "taken out" then your role was passed immediately onto your 2ic (second in charge) to carry on. If the 2ic died, it went to their 3ic understudy and so on. The continuity of a chain of command ensures survival and seamless operations under difficult situations.

It was not a luxury to have this structure, this chain had to be identified and developed. From the regiment's commanding officer to the cooks, key positions were always responsible for identifying and training an understudy.

I believe succession planning will be a significant challenge our industry will face in the coming years. The baby boomers will be leaving the industry and with them will go the accumulated knowledge and practises of many years. To ensure we survive and operate seamlessly we too need to be grooming our 2ic candidates.

At LAMP conference a few years ago in Atlanta, I randomly polled field managers and leaders asking them what they would do if key people left their branch or agency suddenly. Often the answer came, "When you get right down to it, we really have no plan" or "I guess everyone would have to share the load and work harder until the right person was found" or "I'm not worrying about it, that's head office's job!"

It's been said that advisors bring in the business but managers build the agency. That being said, everyone is replaceable. While the decision may not lie entirely with you, I bet you'd prefer to have intelligent input for this inevitable situation.

Identify candidates early; during advisor selection let them know there are manager opportunities within your company for good candidates. Have a candidate pool to pick from, enjoy the opportunity to choose a great manager candidate from several good candidates. Having your agency known as a place to grow and cultivate leadership talent is complimentary of your agency culture and professionalism. There is nothing wrong with having many great leaders originating from your agency to take other positions within the company and industry. Build a legacy bigger than yourself and your branch.

In the Army, the chances of getting literally "taken out" were a reality. For you, we're not talking death necessarily; but what about retirement, an opportunity for your spouse that requires a move to another city, or a long-term disability or illness in your family?

What does the ideal candidate look like? Create a "shopping list" of attributes and accomplishments that may include individuals who are good mentors, possess recruiting skills and high energy, common sense, industry designations and achievements, community involvement, etc. Perhaps ask a trusted colleague what core competencies they think would make a good successor for you or a needed talent set for your agency. Listen to them, their objectivity to the situation could be, well… enlightening.

Your successor doesn't have to be a clone of you. Don't take this personally; everything you brought to the table got the branch to where it is today, however, the next leap forward may require a different paradigm. Be open to this.

Start looking in your own backyard first: your agency, your management team, your peers, or talk to your VP (chances are this person is already a couple steps ahead of you on this matter). These people are familiar with the systems and cultures this person will be entering into from a perspective outside your own. If these resources don't generate at least three to five good prospects then start looking elsewhere. Does everyone in your personal and professional world know you are looking for a prodigy or successor? If not, book some coffee chats with colleagues and COIs.

If you find someone that fits the bill but you (or the candidate) want to wait until they are completely ready to take the next position here's a suggestion; rethink that. They will never be completely ready for the next step. Do you remember your first few months as a new sales manager or branch manager? No matter how much you knew going into the new role, it was still like drinking from a fire hose. And if you strive for more in your career likely you are still learning concepts, methods, and strategies that will improve your skills. Therefore, if the person who hired you waited until they thought you were completely ready to take that new role you'd probably still be waiting where you were.

The need for succession planning happens on two occasions: a) when you are ready, and b) when you're not.

Pick the first one.

New Year Launch Letter - Example

A very well received idea we did a couple of years ago started out as simply a fun thing to do for a couple of agents who said they wanted a boost of self-esteem before walking into the New Year. We developed a simple letter outlining why this particular agent was a good person to meet with at the beginning of the year. Printed on letterhead and signed by the branch manager, agents distributed these letters to their block of clients in both paper and digital formats. It took a bit of time to generate the template but the production results for the agents have been outstanding.

(Date)

Special Announcement for (agent name)

> Advisor photo

It is my pleasure to announce that (name) has achieved a Gold Level status of national recognition for his hard work and service to clients in 2016. He has earned a place with the top financial advisors within our office and region. My sincere appreciation and congratulations go out to (agent name) and his wife (name) for an amazing 2016.

In the last year, (name) has become a leader within our office and continues to develop himself for the benefit of his business and the clients he cares about. This year he started his Certified Financial Professional (CFP) designation to expand his knowledge and abilities further. His client service standards are excellent, and this is shown through outstanding client retention and loyalty seen year after year. (name's) passion for ongoing excellence and learning is also apparent; he started his wealth practise in 2014 as well as becoming one of top health advisors last year.

Over the last three years, (name) has become a very trusted and valued member of our team here at our agency. In 2014, it was announced that our office was named one of the top branches in Canada for production, business quality, and consistent growth in our community; (name) was a significant part of that achievement. As much as he touches the hearts of his colleagues, I know he is valued and respected in his community equally.

I wish (name) continued success and trust that he will continue to shine as one of best and brightest stars here at our branch.

Greg Powell
Branch Manager

Working With Generation Y Agents

Like me, you may have some framed certificates or awards on your walls. And also like me, these hanging frames may be used to cover something: a small hole or unsightly scuff mark perhaps. One of my frames hides a forehead-sized dent produced from repeatedly pounding my noggin against the wall after dealing with people who may bring the biggest opportunity and cause for change in our industry: the Y Generation.

You have met this perplexing group before; the young guns whose production highs and lows can give you whiplash but cause them no concern, who arrive at the office wearing designer jeans and white shoes, who talk about ethical funds and video games, who work three 18-hour days in a row with four-day weekends, and who often can't return your phone calls but update their Facebook page every 15 minutes.

Many industries, including financial services, are feeling the Gen Y presence and influence in the workplace. It is paramount we understand the impact this group will have and ensure we aren't left behind. At the 2009 Leadership Conference, Advocis had Intergen Consulting Group provide special workshops for our leaders to learn and bring the information back to their workplaces. We need to understand this group we'll eventually pass the industry over to.

Born generally between 1980 and 1994, with the lowest parent-to-child ratio in history, this group was raised in their own unique era filled with defining moments in history that have impacted them greatly (9-11, YouTube, and the economic crash of 2008). They are the most racially and ethnically diverse generation in history and the most educated group to date with over 60 percent attending some post-secondary. They possess an unquenchable thirst for the "new," reared in a button-click world of instant gratification and probably had their first smartphone before their first kiss.

Recruiting

Being highly social, you can attract this group through technology and social media like Facebook. Reaching candidates through personal, not business, connections works best with this cohort. Learn their language and preferred means of communicating with you (i.e. texting, Skype, Twitter, and FaceTime) and use it.

During selection interviews emphasize satisfaction and balance, let them know what they do is meaningful work. They are content to keep changing jobs until they find one that aligns with their personal and professional goals. They want success but are not willing to work 60 hours a week to get it. Tell them the truth; don't try to get them excited as they can smell hype versus substance.

Training

Ask them what their goal is, ask why this goal is important, and then offer direction on how to achieve it. They can be high achievers who have benefited from parental guidance in their lives and thrive on concrete milestones. Eventually they will make the process their own but initially they want YOU to show them how. When confronted with unclear guidelines or minimal management, Gen Y's tend to flounder.

Provide constant feedback; they are used to an instantaneous world, high rates of information, and individualized attention. One-on-one mentoring communicates a sense of caring and instills a sense of loyalty to the manager providing it. The phrase "complimenting them into success" comes to mind here.

Being better educated than previous generations, Gen Y's expect to be taught well and being given the right tools. Clear and comprehensive training programs, mentoring opportunities, and continuing education (CE or PACE) credits through such things as podcasts and webinars are sought after. They can process vast amounts of information; provide it or they will seek it elsewhere.

Remember they are "hands-on" as well as visual learners because of their comfort and use of technology. They may want to continue learning well after the office's training room is closed for the day. Access to on-line learning and courses-on-demand systems is important to work with their schedule to study products and sales concepts.

Retention

This group doesn't quit the job; they quit the manager. Model the behaviour you want from them and you will see better results than telling them to shape up. Allow them the flexibility you talked about during your first interviews, little things like socially networking at work can go a long way.

Make the workplace fun and put them on teams. They enjoy achievements as a group, being praised publicly, as opposed to being individual performers. They have been raised as part of a network—technologically and socially—so working together breeds creativity and satisfaction. Recruit groups of these people at once. Introduce them to one another early in the process and let them get their licenses and training together.

For recognition, immediacy is key. Don't be surprised if one of your Gen Y agents texts you with a sale they just closed or a great meeting they just had with a COI. They are rightfully proud of their win, text back immediately congratulating them on their success. At the end of a day, look at the sales made by this group and recognize each one by Twitter or Facebook.

Managers who have succeeded to this point in managing by intimidation and threats won't make it with this generation. This is a generation that has never known unemployment. Money isn't the prime motivator and unlike previous generations that grumble but stay for the sake of a paycheque, Gen Y's won't put up with it. Often they choose you, not the other way around, and will constantly re-assess whether to stay with your organization.

The Journey from Recruiting to Training to Retention

A colleague of the philosopher Ludwig Wittgenstein once stated, "What a bunch of idiots the people hundreds of years ago must have been when they thought the Sun revolved around the Earth when everyone knows it's the other way around." To which Ludwig replied, "Yeah, but imagine what it would have looked like if the Sun had revolved around the Earth." The point being of course it would have looked exactly the same. We see what we want to see. Perceptions command reality.

You believe your agency or branch is supportive, efficient, and delivers on all important areas of your advisor's careers. That is your reality because that's how you see the organization (one you've had a part in building I might add). If the advisors say, or show, they aren't experiencing sufficient levels of support to get what they need from you to be successful then that's their reality. And it's just as valid, and real, as yours.

Why do clients stay with certain advisors and not with others? Clients see value in keeping good business relationships, even though rough times happen and they could get similar services from many other sources. The same is true for your advisors; they will only stay if they see value in doing so. The grass-is-greener phenomenon occurs all the time but it certainly hurts when someone leaves because of it.

When we have the sometimes-uncomfortable "goodbye" conversations with advisors, the primary reasons for them leaving the industry include quality of advisor, lack of production (and therefore income), lack of training and support, their market is exhausted, etc. Some secondary reasons for leaving can include a significant conflict with another advisor, frustration over how the agency does something, or simply not knowing how to run their business properly. If they mention these, dig a little deeper in your conversation as you may be able to turn the conversation around.

Retention starts at your first meeting

The passion to be an entrepreneur and help others becomes evident quickly in the interviewing and selection process.

Offering sales call "ride-alongs" during pre-contract or organizing interviews with advisors already in your office give realistic expectation of what they will earn initially, and being extremely clear on the challenges of the business are paramount to avoid shock in the role later on. Do this before offering them a position and don't gloss over the difficulties they will experience. They will find out soon enough how tough this career is, and they may resent it if they feel you never told them.

Fulfilling on the promises made during selection

During our first meetings with a candidate, they will usually weave into the conversation three questions: how do I get paid, where will I find my clients, and how will you train and support me? How accurately you answer these questions will put you both on a longer career path.

Don't let them, or you, off the hook on these points after the initial months of training and setting them loose into the wild. Have a structured training system taking them into their second year and include getting additional licenses and designations such as CFP into their plan. If you take a genuine interest in their career beyond the production they generate they will appreciate it.

Offer specialized training for different groups of agents in your office, not only your new advisors. Veteran advisors are often a group that gets missed because they run a steady business and don't knock on your door too often any more. If you have a sub-group of advisors that show aptitude for affluent markets, group benefits, or high-end wealth then perhaps open a monthly peer-to-peer forum and organize guest speakers for these topics.

Mentoring opportunities

Try your best to arrange a mentoring relationship for every new advisor you bring in. Peer-to-peer accountability is often stronger than anything managers can apply. Where possible align the mentor and mentee in regard to language, market access, personality, and sometimes even age. Often people look to this career because it's meaningful work and has tremendous income potential but it's important to never lose sight that it's still a sales career. Often a rookie agent will tell a peer or colleague more about their challenges than they will ever tell their recruiter or coaching manager. If you have good relationships with the mentors then you will have access to subtlety address potential problems before they turn into big ones.

Learning takes place in the field far more effectively than it occurs in the training room. Joint fieldwork shows new advisors how to do the job in the real world. As much as you know about selling financial products, your top advisors know more. They will help rookies increase productivity, manage expenses and revenues like a start-up business should, teach cross-sell techniques within their market, and confide they too hate asking for referrals but do it anyway because it's important.

Remember that new advisors will become mentors and "veterans" in as little as three to five years. Establish standards for qualifying for your office's mentor program and remind members of your agency often. Create interest in the agency for joining the group of mentors, perhaps even have a quarterly mentor group lunch to discuss the mentees performance and brainstorm ideas to help them.

Culture is the glue that makes them sticky

Having an agency calendar of fun social events allows advisors and their families to bond in a non-work environment. The connections between VIP's, spouses and their children is healthy and essential to build a strong culture, the natural by-product will be the feeling of deepening roots into the agency. If you're not good at planning such activities, or would like to start a social committee to organize these events, appoint a manager on your team along with interested advisors to be its nucleus. Managers should be involved but the purpose of the social committee should remain "by advisors for advisors" and not another mandatory branch event.

Involve the advisors' spouses in as many agency activities as possible such as recognition events and even AGMs. You can host specific appreciation events for the spouses and assistants to recognize their behind-the-scenes efforts and support. Remember it's them the advisors vent to when having a tough day.

An advisor you don't lose is one you don't have to replace through the long and winding path of recruiting. Anything you can add to show value to your advisors will make them "sticky" to your organization. If they feel active, happy, and successful, they will stay longer.

The Secret to Increasing Self-confidence

Andrew Barber-Starkey

There are few things that are more important to a financial professional than confidence. The confidence to set the appointments, to close for a sale, ask for referrals or—as far as that goes—get what you want in any area of your life.

But how do you increase confidence? Is there a formula that will work every time, without fail, to leave you feeling stronger and better about yourself?

As it turns out, there IS a formula.

It was years ago but I will never forget that moment. I walked into the kitchen and my wife had the radio on and was listening to radio therapist, Dr. Laura. On the line was a young woman who was crying and whimpering about how bad her life was with men and so on. Dr. Laura said to her, *"Young lady, what you need is more confidence."* The caller surprised me with her response. She said, *"I know. But how do I get more confidence?"*

Being a coach, I waited with great anticipation for Dr. Laura's response. Her simple answer was "I can tell you how to get more confidence in two words: *Impress yourself.*"

It took me a moment to realize that Dr. Laura had hit the nail on the head. You see, most of us spend our time, effort, and money trying to impress other people. We believe that other people's approval will validate us and make us feel better about ourselves. But the truth is that confidence and self-esteem are an inside job. It is what YOU think of yourself that matters. In fact impressing other people sometimes undermines your self-confidence, because deep down it can make you feel like a fraud.

Your confidence increases each time you prove to yourself that YOU can trust yourself. Each time you impress yourself with an action you take, your self-image receives a boost. If you impress yourself repeatedly, your self-image will become stronger and you will reap the rewards both internally and externally.

How to Avoid the Pitfalls

Here are some ways you may inadvertently be diminishing your self-confidence:

1) Comparing yourself to others
If you are like most people, you look to see how you compare to others and judge yourself accordingly. The problem is that you will always see yourself as better than some people but not as good as others. You must learn to view others as not better or less than you but simply as different.

2) Judging yourself by other people's opinions
One way to feel great about yourself is to be true to yourself instead of being concerned with what others think you should do. When you listen to and follow your own inner guidance, your confidence increases. Grammy-winning music producer Quincy Jones had it right when he said, "Not one drop of my self-worth depends on your opinion of me."

3) Defining your self-worth by your performance
Many people, men in particular, have been programmed since childhood to base their self-worth on their ability, productivity, and accomplishments. Impress yourself with who you are, not how much you do.

4) Focusing on failures rather than successes
You have undoubtedly had far more successes than failures. Instead of replaying what didn't work over and over, develop the habit of noticing your progress and successes. This simple shift in attention can literally change your life.

5) Being a perfectionist
Perfectionists have unrealistic expectations of themselves. Nothing is ever good enough. Perfectionists are hard on others but even harder on themselves.

When they fail to achieve their own unreasonable expectations, they beat themselves up mercilessly. This undermines their self-confidence creating a downward spiral that leads to inaction and failure.

How to Build Confidence

Free yourself from the above traps and you will be in a better position to impress yourself. Here are some tips and practises that will help:

1) Take action

When you take action, you will almost always be more impressed with yourself than if you don't take action. Procrastination, over-analyzing, and rationalization usually cause you to be self-critical.

2) Be decisive

Practise making decisions quickly rather than putting them off. Act boldly; take the initiative when opportunities arise.

3) Set goals based on actions instead of results

Most people set goals based what they want to achieve. However, in many cases, especially in sales, getting the results you want is not within your control. The only thing you can control is the actions you take. So state your goals in terms of the activities you will do and let the results take care of themselves. That way no matter what the outcome, you can win.

4) Keep your agreements with yourself and others

Making a commitment to another person and failing to keep it is a bad thing to do because you lose their trust and damage your reputation with yourself, too. But breaking agreements with yourself is far more damaging because it erodes your self-trust. When you think about it, self-trust and self-confidence is the same thing. Every time you follow through on a commitment you make to yourself, your confidence increases.

5) Be on time

When you are late, how do you feel about yourself? Certainly not impressed. So stop it! In fact try arriving 10 minutes early for all meetings and appointments; it will change your life!

The Ultimate Confidence Building Question

Here is a powerful question you can use in virtually any situation that will help you increase your confidence. Simply ask yourself, "How can I handle this situation in a way that causes me to be impressed with myself?" Listen to the answer inside yourself and follow through with it. Do this and over time your confidence will skyrocket. I know this works because I have done it myself. In fact, I was so impressed with this concept that I bought the website, ImpressYourself.com.

No matter how successful you are today, if you want to achieve bigger goals it is essential that you increase your confidence. True success is being able to look at yourself in the mirror and feel proud of whom you are. The more you impress yourself, the prouder you will feel!

By Andrew Barber-Starkey, Master Certified Coach
Founder and President, The ProCoach Success System

Make a Really Big Deal of a Very Important Anniversary

Neil Hanson

What anniversary may be more important than your birthday? What anniversary may even rank right up there with your wedding anniversary as having had a significant influence on your life? How about your career anniversary?

Most good ideas are plagiarized and I picked this gem up in the eighties when I was a young manager trainee. One of my company's top managers at that time was Mike Young, a successful experienced manager who headed up one of the company's flagship financial centres. At a presentation at a new managers' school Mike shared many great ideas with us. They were simple and easy to implement concepts of his that he said would pay huge dividends in building strong relationships with advisors, contribute to improved advisor retention, and generated advisor referrals.

This is just one of the ideas Mike shared with us that day.

Mike asked us to reflect on the importance of our own decisions to enter the insurance business. For me, the decision to enter this business was a significant leap of faith and I am forever indebted to both the advisor who referred me and the manager who opened my eyes to this career opportunity.

Mike further asked if anyone had made the effort to **make a "big deal"** of our career anniversary. Most of us had to admit that the answer was "No." Mike suggested that we make a big deal out of the career anniversary of every advisor and management team member in our own agencies when we became an agency leader. The idea was simple and easy to implement and, as I learned over the years, well worth the effort. Here's how I adapted Mike's idea to my own operation when I became the head of my agency.

You will need a process to make this work for you and avoid missing anyone's anniversary. Every advisor's anniversary was loaded in the branch calendars and two weeks in advance of the anniversary, my assistant would remind me to send an invitation asking the advisor to join me for their *"career anniversary celebration"* breakfast. I always chose a prestigious location, it was important to make the celebration something to remember.

My last financial centre was in beautiful Victoria, British Columbia and there were many good restaurants from which to choose. If we didn't meet at my club I would reserve a table in a restaurant on the 18th floor of a beautiful downtown hotel that offered a spectacular 270 degree view of our harbour with the Olympic Mountains in the distance. A stunning world-class vista! When the advisor confirmed they were able to meet me, I would make the reservation making a point to request the best table, a corner table with a nice view.

I chose to make it an "Anniversary Breakfast" for all but the quinquennial (recurring every 5 years) anniversaries. For the more significant milestones (fifth, tenth, and other milestone anniversaries) the invitation was for lunch or dinner and, where possible, it would include the advisor's spouse. In both of the financial centres I lead during my years in management, there were advisors who lived in cities some distance from my office. If it were not possible for the advisor to come to me, I would look for the most prestigious location in their city.

My process involved some important preliminary preparation. It starts with a review of notes from the last anniversary celebration I shared with the advisor. Review significant achievements or contributions made by the advisor over the past year, but don't limit it to the last year only. Has the advisor been a formal or informal mentor in the financial centre? What personal or business obstacles have they overcome? What positive part have they played in supporting financial centre culture? Are there any advisors or managers who have joined the financial centre because of this advisor's referral?

The personal part of the file is equally important. What is the spouse's name and career? What are the names and ages of their children and/or grandchildren? What do you know about the advisor's community or church involvement, their hobbies or interests? At the anniversary breakfast, you want conversation to be free flowing and to touch on both the business and personal side of their lives. This should lead to a stronger relationship with the advisor. As your organization grows in size, it becomes increasingly important to complete this review before the meeting, that is, unless unlike me, you have a perfect memory.

This should be all about the advisor, their family, and to celebrate their career and accomplishments. This meeting is not intended to recognize sales achievements. Successful advisors will have received their share of that kind of recognition, income, and lifestyle that accompany sales success. During the meeting, the advisor should feel acknowledged for who they are and not what they have sold. You will be surprised about how much the advisor will open up about themselves, their career, and personal aspirations, and even about the financial centre. The casual informal nature of the meeting makes it a pleasurable experience for you and the advisor.

Make no attempt to turn this into a "selfish" meeting and introduce a business agenda. If it happens naturally, that's OK but is not the objective of this meeting. Afterwards, your process should include making notes of important things requiring follow-up and notes that you will want to review before the next anniversary celebration. Trust me, as the years go on and the anniversaries accumulate you will find these notes to be invaluable.

As your agency operation grows, the anniversary celebration habit will help you stay connected with all your advisors, from the very best to those struggling to be their best. Over the course of my career, I came to learn how much the advisors appreciated the big deal I made of their big day.

Mike Young challenged me to try this for two years. He was convinced that after we make our habits, the habits will make us. Make a big deal of career anniversaries. You have nothing to lose and the potential benefits are huge.

By Neil Hanson CFP, CLU, ChFC, CPCA
38 year Field Manager and large-case coach

The Managers Role in Developing Advisors

Tony Bosch

I've spent the past 25 years working with thousands of advisors. I began as a career agency sales manager then moved to a managing general agency (MGA) principal and now I'm on the executive side. From these experiences, I have learned the importance of the acronym PCPC that represents four can't-fail principles to move an agent's business practise to the next level.

PCPC stands for Purpose, Commitment, Process, and Coachability. Let's break down the principles in more detail and discuss the manager's role in helping their advisors implement these principles successfully.

Purpose: redefine and communicate

Purpose is the starting point. The advisor needs a strong sense of purpose; understanding the need in their uniquely defined market and the belief that they are the most capable person to fill this need is the foundational attitude required for an advisor to survive in our industry. Without it, few advisors will last longer than six to eighteen months.

The challenge for those who have been in the industry for several years, and the reason so many advisors plateau, is that they lose this sense of purpose. They get bogged down in administration, adhering to regulations, and spending time in areas they attempted to escape when joining the industry. This causes them to lose sight of their purpose, eroding their confidence and their drive to pursue higher outcomes.

The manager needs to help the advisors get out of this slump. The first step is encouraging the advisors to do some soul searching and define "why" they are in the business. Who do they feel needs the services they offer? As an entrepreneur, will they be compensated appropriately to create an organization that allows them to fulfill this purpose for others?

It is also an important exercise to have them look outside the industry and explore all the other opportunities that would be available to them. Evaluate the pros and cons of each, thinking through the income earned per hour worked, the flexibility and control of time, the future business potential, and satisfaction. When their research resells them on this career it will result in a rebirth in enthusiasm and drive. The answers to these questions will provide direction for the other decisions they need to make around structure, staffing, resources, and requirements.

The ability to communicate their purpose with sincerity, clarity, and passion will be the most important factor in attracting the right type and quantity of clients necessary to move their practise to the next level. When their "why" is well defined, the "who will benefit" becomes evident. The agent needs to fully understand this when communicating purpose and why people should deal with them. It is important to avoid feeling like a robot providing a monotonous list of products and services to people. Instead, they will realize greater success when they say, "What my clients say I do for them is…" which focuses on the emotional benefit of the outcome of the work they do. This should be modified for each target market the agent decides to work in.

Commitment: assess and define

Commitment starts with an assessment of what price needs to be paid and the willingness to pay that price to fulfill your purpose. These days it seems like everyone you meet has goals to run a marathon, climb Kilimanjaro, or sail across an ocean. Conferences are filled with speakers who have achieved amazing feats of endurance and hardship to accomplish their goals.

Occasionally I get a fleeting thought that maybe I should challenge myself to achieve one of these feats but it does not take long to change my mind once I begin assessing the commitment it would require in preparation, training, and finances. If the pursuit of a goal is not driven by passion, there will be no commitment. A statement starting with "maybe someday" or "maybe I should" lacks commitment. Sadly, many advisors start out with great intentions but their lack of passion and commitment prevent them from accomplishing fundamental proven business strategies such as following an annual planning and quarterly review process. It is much like the marathon runner giving up after only completing five kilometres or the sailor turning back at the first signs of a storm.

A successful sales manager must be able to help their advisors determine if they have the commitment necessary to succeed in this industry. The commitment stage requires a clear understanding of the investment in time, energy, and resources necessary to fulfill the purpose. Once committed, continuing to make choices that will have the greatest impact on achieving that purpose and the resolve to achieve it regardless of the obstacles. Managers should challenge their advisors to answer the questions below as the answers that come from it are vital tools when determining commitment.

- Am I willing to do what is necessary?
- What are the most challenging obstacles I am likely to encounter?
- How have I responded in the past?
- How will I respond differently in the future to achieve the goal?
- What will be the last thing I would do before quitting?

Process: The embodiment of the commitment

The process step turns the decisions made in the commitment stage into successful routines and new habits that replace the need to make moment-by-moment decisions. It requires breaking the commitment into repeatable steps that can be monitored, measured, and modified as needed. These steps, if repeated at a defined level within a defined timeframe, will fulfill the purpose. The processes are followed faithfully with the knowledge they will provide the best possibility of success.

When advisors state they are committed to achieving more, the first questions I urge sales managers to ask them are:

- What is your new process?
- How has it changed from the past process?

- How is it going to generate results?
- At what level?
- And why will it work?

If the replies are vague, the advisor has communicated a non-committal attitude. Every commitment has to be followed by a clear, well-thought-out plan to make the changes necessary to create a new result for them. When motivation and passion wane, sticking to the process keeps the fulfillment of the purpose on course.

Coachability

As Socrates put it, "the key to wisdom is knowing that you do not know." Coachability is the understanding that achieving the best results possible requires teamwork or at least outside input. It means seeking out mentors and being willing to accept direction from others who possess a proven track record. Coachability stems from an internal faith that the purpose is possible and the answers are out there but need to be discovered and applied by continually refining one's processes and therefore reconfirming one's commitment to achieve the best possible outcome. The term also embodies accountability and the willingness to "keep score" to determine if you are on course and to make changes if you are not.

Surprisingly, in my years of experience, I have found this quality the rarest but the most crucial to maximizing agent potential. Most advisors would define themselves as coachable and willingly attend sessions with me and intently answer my questions only to respond with "yes, but ..."

The important question to ask ourselves is not what we know but what have we yet to discover and how finding it might help us achieve our full potential. As sales managers, we look for advisors who are coachable but we should also do some soul searching to see if we ourselves are coachable. We need to encourage our advisors, and ourselves, to ask themselves the following questions:

- Am I willing to seek out what is necessary?
- Will I allow myself to be held accountable?
- Am I willing to accept responsibility for my results and take new actions necessary to get me on course?
- What characteristic, experience do I require in a coach to help me get to the next level?
- Will I invest time and money on a coach?

Following the PCPC principles will provide the foundation for new advisor survival and continued growth throughout their careers. It is vital to help advisors adjust to the many new challenges our industry will face. Overall, I believe a manager needs to both model and promote the PCPC principles, as they are the key to advisors achieving better results with confidence and passion.

By Tony Bosch, CFP, CLU, CH.F.C, CHS, MFA, BA

Executive VP, Broker Development at HUB Financial Inc.

Points to Remember from this Section

1. Income Diversification Elevators
2. Know how to work beside different generations
3. Mid-year recognition letters

Now add points you want to remember and refer back to

-
-
-

My Notes:

_____

_____

_____

_____

_____

_____

_____

Section 4

Keep your Tribe Together

Why We Lose Good Agents

Why do people leave your organization? That's a huge question and one without a single answer. I find it a misunderstood concept that handling retention happens at a specific crisis or event in time. An analogy could be made when providing good service to a valuable client. Attention shouldn't only be paid when they threaten to leave you for a competitor, or at their 10th year anniversary, or when you want them to buy more products. Retention of your advisors and your managers is an on-going challenge and is something you can do continually. Your efforts to keep good people should be just as important as finding new people for your agency. It is the opposite side of the recruiting coin.

From a business planning point of view it's a good practise to estimate losing at least 15 percent to 20 percent per year. While this is a natural part of our sales industry unfortunately, the ones you lose that year often won't be the agents you predict or necessarily want to leave either. Interestingly, I have found that advisor retention and manager retention are about the same percentages and that leaving those roles are for similar reasons. More details on that topic later.

I love using metaphors of combat in my examples, and here is another one for you. The battle happening for talent behind your organization is just as important as the battlefield you are dealing with in front of you. Focussing only on one side of the conflict leaves you vulnerable to have more casualties than you should and too many losses could mean losing the war.

There are some key times when you can pay particular attention to them that can aid in them staying. Inevitably, some good agents will slip through the cracks or find a legitimately better opportunity with another company. However, I find that many good agents leave us simply because we didn't "street proof" them enough for the challenges and influences that will undoubtedly be ahead of them in a career in the financial services industry.

Virtually all sales organizations have a well-designed and all-consuming recruiting process, whether at the corporate or branch level. Unfortunately, I rarely if ever see a similar enthusiasm or structured retention process in the organizations or agencies I visit. Why this is the case still baffles me but assume that someone at our respective head offices has crunched the numbers and deduced it's better to focus keeping recruits coming through the front door versus watching the back door.

Every advisor that you don't lose is one you don't have to recruit and replace. At the end of the day, would you rather keep the people that you obviously saw potential in during the selection process or spent a lot of time training and coaching only to lose them to winds of adversity, or worse, a competitor who also saw their potential but attracted them away?

By keeping those agents in your organization, you are able to reap the benefits of their past and future production, their residual commissions, and their participation in your agency's culture. They chose and stuck with you for certain reasons and whether it was recognition, your compensation model, your leadership style, or the working environment they are still with you today. Like the beginnings of a personal relationship, at some point you both found it desirable and valuable to be together. Therefore, it's not too late to make some changes to your retention strategy to ensure you have the best chance they stay with you in the future.

The good news is that agents don't necessarily want to throw this working relationship away either. They too have a lot at stake in what they have built with your agency. Unfortunately, there are many influences, both external and internal, to your agency's effort that always try to pull your agents away.

As many of us have encountered while trying to grow our organizations, there are companies in our very competitive industry that particularly target existing advisors to expand their sales force. They do not find or develop their own agents as a predominant growth strategy but will essentially attract advisors from fellow organizations. To be fair, sometimes agents can "outgrow" the situation they currently work in and it is a good thing for them to move on for their business to flourish, other times sharks smell blood in the water and will pick off the struggling fish when they are most vulnerable.

I suppose in a way this method is easier than prospecting, selecting, background checking, identifying market, licensing, training, and coaching these talented people while refining their business practises during the initially difficult years. But if you make a parallel to an agent's world, imagine doing everything an agent does to prospect, define client's needs and budget, work through applications and underwriting, service and support the client over decades only to have someone scoop the client away. Agents in this situation would get understandably frustrated; the same is true for field managers when they lose an agent. But if a client or agent leaves, despite what enticement the outside entity is offering, it is an indication that there is an opportunity to refine their retention processes. As managers, agents are our clients. You will lose some along the way and that's normal. If you perceive you are losing too many then you can do something about it.

Whether a competitor offers the advisor freedom to make their own website or a large signing bonus it can NOT add up to everything you have done to get them to a place where they are now considered attractive to this other party. This is why it hurts when they go.

Sometimes these forces will talk to anyone with the requisite licenses, other times they target specific companies or agencies because they train good agents. Why spend all the time and effort cultivating their own crops when they can simply go over to your farmland and put your corn in their pick-up and drive away?

It sounds horrible doesn't it? Similar situations happen to all of us over the years but at the end of the day the only way they can attract your people is when they are "attractable." At our branch, I have had several incidents where competitors had people literally planted inside my office trying to recruit my agents away. The first time this happened there was some damage done and several advisors left, but afterwards we changed our retention strategies and we were able to minimize scenarios like this happening again.

The common methods used by many competing financial sales companies to "fish" for agents are largely unsuccessful such as email blasts, invitation letters, cold phone calls to their work number, and seemingly harmless "educational" webinars.

If you have a good connection to the people within your agency, your advisors will often forward you the email received or give you the letter to look over. Thank these advisors when they do this, as they are under no obligation to alert you. They obviously care about the organization, see value in staying, and also deem this approach a bit dubious. This is a great opportunity to connect with people you deem at risk because they likely received the same solicitation.

In the financial services industry retention is less than 18 percent at the four-year benchmark in North America, with the majority of agents leaving in the 2nd and 3rd years. So what does this percentage actually mean? This year if your agency recruits 10 agents then four years from now only about 2 agents will still be with your organization from that year's cohort. What is a little misleading, however, is that many are likely still practicing as financial sales representative after they left your agency. They are still productive agents for the industry; they just aren't doing it with your company's logo on their business card. If that's so, then an opportunity to retain them with your organization could have been missed.

People on the outside of the industry may remark how low the retention rates are and therefore must be proof that the industry isn't very professional or attract high-quality individuals. This perception couldn't be further from the truth. This number is comparable or better than other sales industries such as mortgage brokers, high-end automobile salespeople, and full-time real estate agents. I would say it would stand up against the initial candidates starting medical or legal professions who are still working with their first career institution after four years. I'd be curious what the percentages would look like for shopping mall retail workers, warehouse employees, or even soldiers for four-year retention with the initial employer. I hate to say it but some people won't stay with your company no matter what you do. However, to add insult to injury, some agents will stay with your organization for years after they should have moved onto another career.

I don't believe our industry should strive for 100 percent even if it's theoretically possible. But what if you could increase your agency's retention numbers by 100 percent? Say, from 18 percent to 36 percent? If your agency could do that, even if 64 percent don't make it to the fourth year you would be a leader in this metric. Moreover, the demand for new recruits at the front-end would lessen a bit allowing you to select and train even better.

Not everybody who starts a career in this field will make it despite the best intentions of management or the individuals themselves. It happens sometimes; some retire, some have a health incident, some have their spouse get a job in another city, and so on. Let's face it, it's a commissioned sales occupation so not everybody is cut out for it and that's normal. Not everybody is cut out to be a soldier either but at the end of the day some can stick it out by just standing still, shutting up, holding a rifle, wear green khakis, and waiting for someone to tell them what to do. Yet other people want to excel in their careers, get promoted, and make their mark on their chosen field.

Retention is really about continually re-recruiting an agent after they have gone through all obstacles and have contracted with your company. There are many opportunities to re-recruit at key moments of recognition where you're taking them out for an anniversary lunch or celebration involving the whole branch. You can reinforce to them why they took a leap of faith and got into the business. "Congratulations, Stan! I remember a year ago when I first met you and Samantha and you were concerned about earning enough income. Look at what you have accomplished, look at the lifestyle you have provided for your family. Wow, what's the next step in your career? You were really interested in development, maybe this year is an opportunity to take a look at your Certified Financial Planner designation."

Particularly if they're challenge motivated or development motivated, you can re-recruit them as there is no limit to the success you can have in this industry and designations abound. There are also specific benchmarks around the two, three, and four-year mark where many advisors have a kind of identity crisis about the career. "I've made it in the career so far. It's going OK and I enjoy parts of the career but do I see myself doing this forever? Maybe I need a change or a fresh start to reboot myself?"

Those are the moments that happen to us all at one time or another. A good colleague of mine, who I called for some venting after having a particularly challenging day, humorously called these moments "quitting days." These days are when you put your job or career under a microscope to recheck your satisfaction against the rewards, effort, stress, etc. you feel. These times are normal and healthy for managers and agents but unfortunately more often occur when a person feels "down" and not "up" in their careers.

We usually get through these intense introspection flashes and remain where we are. Sometimes using a mentor or other objective sounding board who knows you well is a good reaction to deal with these days. They can often keep your feet on the ground, commiserate a little bit, and remind you of all the reasons why you should look forward to a fresh start tomorrow. My friend did say, however, that too many of these "quitting days" in a row could be a real indicator that where you are is no longer where you may want to be.

Sometimes it can be an approach letter from a competing organization that is sitting on their desk since last week. Or a friend meeting you for coffee saying "Oh, you're still doing that eh? It sure sounds difficult. Maybe you could take what you learned and try something slightly different?" Or a normally supportive spouse can spot an advertisement in the local newspaper announcing another financial company that operates a bit closer to home. Rather than nudging the agent to stick with it at their career's tipping point, they nudge them out. It doesn't take much to plant a seed, or make them open to thinking about it.

This battle to retain agents will happen every day in your hallways. It is moments like these you'll be thankful you have a retention strategy, or in military terms "harden the target," to withstand constant bombardment that assail good agents.

Motivation – What Drives Your Agents?

Too often managers make quick assumptions about potential candidates regarding what their motivations are. My own experience as a junior manager was that I was told by those senior to me that motivation in my candidates would likely be money. However, I tried to approach my candidates differently, choosing instead to listen to their stories and ask, "What's important to you."

I learned candidates are motivated to come into this business for more than just money. The motivations range from being able to attend their kid's piano recital without having to beg for time off, wanting to leave legacy after they retire, to be running their own business, to being in a professional career, and yes, sometimes it's income too. Before a manager begins to "fish" for candidates to potentially enter the career, they might want to know what the fish are interested in. To choose the proper lure one needs to know their personal motivation.

What motivates people to be an agent?

Often people are attracted to the financial services industry because they are not getting what they want with their current occupation or work environment. Most of us, myself included, fresh out of high school did not rush to the burgeoning lineup of enthusiastic candidates to join the ranks of self-employment selling insurance and investments.

Candidates are motivated by a wide variety of drivers and they can change with maturity. This is not an exhaustive list but includes common categories I see. During an initial interview, the clock is ticking loudly in your ear counting down your 30-minute commitment to them. Therefore, any heuristics to quickly compartmentalize potential candidates quickly is likely appreciated. By learning these broad categories you will be able to identify within minutes what drives the candidate. Evidently, since they are talking to you, they feel their driver is not being addressed by their current job. They are able to look at our industry and explore something they never knew existed.

I've found some markets tend to cluster around specific motivations, such as single parents and the opportunity for flexibility. It should be said that a candidate can have more than one motivator (in varying degrees) and it can even be dependent on a specific arena of their life. Someone can be challenge motivated in a sport, but security motivated at work.

Challenge Motivated

These people are stimulated by what is difficult; they like to succeed at what other people perceive as tough. I've always liked Winston Churchill's quote "if you find yourself going through hell, keep on going." Find someone who likes the idea of walking through the fire to be one of the few who make it to the other side and they will be someone motivated by challenge.

Some just like to be stimulated, to be told a task is near impossible or at least one that would make most people pale at the thought. This driver motivates athletes that want to be in the top 1 percent of their sport to salespeople who want to be in the winner's circle at a convention. These people love their feet hitting the bedroom carpet in the morning knowing they can do something most others can't, or won't. This "elitism" turns them on, and I put myself in this category. Maybe it's a throwback from my military days but I love knowing I did things that other people would simply not be capable of doing, often they can barely imagine it when I talk about it. The same can be said of what drives firefighters and police officers. It's the fight that gets our engines revving and being in our industry can be just like that!

Who are the 'Challenge-motivated' agents in my office?

Name	What can I do to fire them up?
1.	
2.	
3.	
4.	
5.	

Income Motivated

This term is largely self-explanatory: the candidate is currently not making enough income to provide for the lifestyle they desire. Perhaps this candidate doesn't feel the efforts and skill they put into their current job provides appropriate compensation: a perceived disparity of work given to income provided. Other candidates actually are making a good income but they just want more than they had last year: more success, more vacation days, more money, bigger house, or a nicer car.

If you think they are motivated by money, don't make an assumption. Ask, "What would be a good income for you?" When they give you a big number, ask, "When would you like to see that?" If they want that in the first year, then work backwards with them regarding what production level they would need to make that happen. Ask, "Do you want a stable income or a no glass ceilings income?" Regardless of their answer be careful not to impose what you think they should expect, tell the rookie what needs to be done to achieve his goal and let them try!

One can argue it is subtle programming by media and magazines or just the western phenomenon of "keeping up with the Jones." There is an unending desire in many to have more than they had last year and this is usually tied to disposable income. At the end of the day, everything is driven by income: from paying down the mortgage to investment plans to buying groceries. While income doesn't necessarily make happiness, it does provide more options in life than those without it: university education for the kids, a sunny vacation every year, etc. Maybe simply having these options may make that person feel happy. One warning though; this type of person can be attracted to "grass is greener" issues, watch they don't leave you for another agency or industry they believe will leapfrog them to the next tax bracket.

Who are the 'Income-motivated' agents in my office?

Name	What can I do to fire them up?
1.	
2.	
3.	
4.	
5.	

Security Motivated

I'm not talking about people who want security in the sense of a guaranteed paycheque every week and want stable benefits. I'm talking about candidates who want control of their career and they don't want someone else making a decision for their career again. I find this motivation is particularly prevalent with people who have been downsized. They had no control over what they did, how much they earned, or even if they would have a job after something happened to their employing company, whether by merger or a dramatic change in the markets. These people worked diligently and loyally for a company for many years only to be told they or their co-workers or even their entire floor is no longer required. They take their package and off they go; and they had a vision of themselves being with the company until they got the gold watch. Unfortunately, it doesn't always end that way. Traditional employment equals no control, period. Employees don't have control of anything: benefits, pensions, income, promotion, or even where they work.

Employees have no real control of their work situation. I'm sorry if that statement hurts their feelings, it's the truth. If a person is an employee, they have no control over their employment status. It will be decided by somebody else, whether the new owner or the comptroller or their department supervisor; they really don't have as much control as a self-employed person. Another part of that security is to have a job that they can have for a long time.

Some give up control for the misguided belief of not being fired from their job ever. These people think, "as long as I show up Monday to Friday and do an OK job I will get benefits and an annual 2 percent salary increase." I'd rather be shot. A government employee may think as long as they do their job they are "unfireable." Wrong! Self-employed people are "unfireable." A good selling feature for our industry is that our business is here forever. You will always be indispensable in this industry, our roles will not fall out of fashion as being an insurance agent has never been in fashion to begin with.

Who are the 'Security-motivated' agents in my office?

Name	What can I do to fire them up?
1.	
2.	
3.	
4.	
5.	

Recognition Motivation

This is the most common driver I come across. These candidates have had success in sports, a previous successful sales career, or worked somewhere where they were "employee of the month" and they discovered they liked the taste of it. When discussing this piece, tell them you want them to be direct and honest in their answers. Don't tell me what you think I want to hear, tell me what truly makes a day feel good for you, because if I know what that is, I can honestly answer back if this career will offer what you need.

These candidates are fueled by recognition and appreciation. If they don't get this often enough it can feel like a large hole in their current career situation. Likely, that's why they are looking to explore other opportunities and are talking to you now. They likely understand that commission-driven roles are full of recognition and incentives: from campaigns to conventions, from reward trips to engraved trophies! When you do a good job in our world, you are sent to places like Cancun and Paris; that is simply not available to an employee in a cubicle occupation. To the winner go the spoils!

Recognition means different things to different people. Find out what recognition means to each candidate and agent you want to impact. Being recognition motivated can be anything from getting a trophy to sit on their desk to being taken out to a wonderful dinner with their spouse. Other times they just wanted to be shown off as the best in a large public setting or a newspaper ad showing their community what they had accomplished. Some people are "badge collectors," possessing a Cub Scout mentality like me. When I was a developing SCUBA diver, I would take another certification every three to four months. I loved stitching my new certification patch onto my diver duffle bag.

People driven by this motivator strive to win an achievement that separates them from their peer group, even for a short amount of time. Recognition-motivated agents are great for this industry because you don't have to spend a lot of money to do recognition well; it's creative and it's fun to celebrate with them and it can motivate others in the room simply by watching them get their shiny trophy.

Who are the 'Recognition-motivated' agents in my office?

Name	What can I do to fire them up?
1.	
2.	
3.	
4.	
5.	

Development Motivation

Some candidates in their current occupation do not feel they are developing in their capabilities year after year, or even after decades. What skills they brought to the table at their current job is exactly where they were ten years ago. They have not changed or evolved. Sometimes that can be attached to an education, degree, or a designation that let them do more advanced projects than their peers. Some people are truly motivated by this while others would rather stick their tongues into an electrical socket.

You can hear the frustration in their voices when they interview with you. They got their current job 15 years ago but after 780 forty-hour workweeks, they have gotten nowhere. They do that job, commute home, have dinner, watch some TV, and go to bed. They desperately want to feel that they are sharpening their skills and improving themselves: they know deep down they should be farther ahead than where they are today. These people are driven by learning and stimulated by absorbing new ideas. These people tend to be voracious readers and the kind of person that will work very hard to be invited to a two-day estate-planning workshop. For these people who excel in sales campaigns or monthly incentives offer them development opportunities to be even better, a day job shadowing a hall of fame agent, or provide a gift certificate for their next career course.

Sub-set: Title Motivated

A perfect example is my former military career where the rank on someone's arm told you exactly what you needed to know about them, how to behave, who to listen to, and who not to make eye contact with.

In our industry, once in a while you see people motivated to become a "manager" or "director" or have a CFP designation on their card, not because they are necessarily interested in being a manager or financial planner, they just like the title. If you give them a fancy sounding title, whether Marketing Manager, Compliance Officer, Sales Manager, or Senior Specialist, they are happy! Right?

Faker Alert! Sometimes people are motivated by title alone and don't want to put in the effort to achieve it or perhaps their passion is more having the role than doing the role. I would recommend you stay away from these managers as you can learn virtually nothing from them but they will gladly consume your time.

Who are the 'Development-motivated' agents in my office?

Name	What can I do to fire them up?
1.	
2.	
3.	
4.	
5.	

Work-Life Balance Motivation

Often times the motivation to change careers is control. These people want control of vacations and to be present for important family moments, or to focus more on personal matters. The work/life balance is often a double-edged sword: working too much leads to burnout, but working too little leads to being out of business. The trick with having a work/life balance is you have to do the first part: you have to do the work!

Golfing does not equal effective prospecting neither do dinners or drinks at bars. I sometimes see agents with less than two years in the business taking as much time off as agents with ten times the seniority! You can certainly go to the gym every day and pick up kids from school but you have to earn a living too. Behaving like someone who is retired doesn't make sense, even under the banner of work/life balance.

Flexibility can be very important for the Gen Y, female and single parent markets. Simply having the ability to control your own work schedule is a luxury many do not enjoy. Perhaps these agents prefer not to have weekend shifts, or if they want two weeks off not to have to beg for permission, or desire to work on evenings and weekends to accommodate a spouse's work schedule. For those with families they may want to drop off the kids at school, or be there for recitals or making the time to take care for an aging parent.

This kind of flexibility is incredibly motivating for modern families including the fast-paced sandwich generation where you take care of not only your children but sometimes your parents too. The normal post-industrial revolution workweek of Monday to Friday sometimes means you sacrifice some work/life balance because you cannot control your time.

Who are the 'Work/Life Balance-motivated' agents in my office?

Name	What can I do to fire them up?
1.	
2.	
3.	
4.	
5.	

In summary, all motivators have a common denominator: it is about control. People that are income motivated like control over their income. They do not want to work their 'nose to the grindstone' for years hoping to get a basic inflation increase or an annual bonus of $500. For people that are security motivated, they want to know they are in control their career; not someone else. With lack of control, many don't feel the motivation. Why would they push harder for a company that does not develop, recognize, and pay them sufficiently day after day, year after year? Asking lots of open-ended questions gives give you information about their personal motivators. Once you discover what type of control they want illustrate how your career opportunity can provide it to them. It's not much harder than that.

Motivation Self-analysis

Here is a chance to do an exercise for yourself, and of course be honest. No one is going to check your answers! I'll go first.

Parallels to military career that finally won me over to this career:

1. Meaningful work – What we do is important to people.
2. Challenge – Most people are not able to do what we do successfully.
3. Development – I'm constantly perfecting my craft.

Why did YOU get into the industry?
1.
2.
3.

Why did YOU become a sales manager?
1.
2.
3.

What inspires YOU to take the next step in your career progression?

1.

2.

3.

Scalable Strategies to Retain Agents in the 21st Century

Growing sales production year after year, increasing agency revenues, and having a dynamic culture largely comes from building your agency bigger every year. By keeping good agents versus continually replacing them is a strategy to do just that. In this piece, we will explore two truths of growth in the financial industry in 2016:

1. The formula for agency growth is more agents IN than OUT.
2. A hard-won agent we KEEP is an agent we don't have to REPLACE through recruiting.

It's my privilege to be the custodian of one of the strongest agencies in Canada in measurements of production, consistent recruiting growth, and quality agent retention. But this was not always the case; earlier in the agency we shrank by 1/3 despite our best recruiting efforts. Some left the financial services industry completely but, unfortunately, some just left us.

We put changes into effect in 2009 that significantly influenced the retention of advisors and put us on a path to keeping our successful agents longer. We are still benefiting from those changes today and I want to share those changes with you.

A leader once said to me "By seeing challenges around you that break your heart, you will find a passion to pursue the solutions." I see good advisors and managers leaving our agencies, this breaks my heart. There is a challenge that persists in not only my own organization but throughout our industry in Canada and US, and one that may only get more profound in the years ahead with the dramatic changes in the available workforce pool.

More than ever, it's important for our collective success in the decades ahead to retain:

1. Field managers who will grow our agencies through recruiting and agent development despite a shrinking available workforce and who provide ongoing leadership to our organizations.

2. Agents who drive distribution of financial security to our citizens, provide manager bench strength, and ensure industry longevity through succession planning in upcoming years.

By "re-recruiting" agents at timely intervals in their career and addressing motivators that made them initially start an agent career, you can provide an adequate defence against both internal and external forces that pull good agents away from your organization. Let us discuss scalable strategies and step-by-step ideas that can help make your people sticky for years to come.

Most of us have heard the retention statistics put out by LIMRA in 2014, which are very useful as general information but it only measures agents leaving their current company. These types of reports do not show the difference from agents leaving a company in favour of another versus those leaving the industry altogether.

North America's financial industry fourth year retention is an average of 18 percent combined (13 percent for agencies under 2,000 agents and 27 percent for larger career models. Our agency has a 4th year retention of 70 percent of full-time 100 percent commissioned agents, that's triple the best out there.

Should we keep 100 percent of all advisors contracted? Of course not. It's not healthy or likely as it is a sales profession after all, but if your agency currently has a 4th year retention of 20 percent, can you have a 100 percent increase to 40 percent? Yes, you can!

If you have chosen to pick up this book (and have read this far to get to this section) then I suspect you're interested in retaining more agents in your organization so I don't have to sell you on the importance. By implementing retention systems as part of your agency's growth strategy, you can double your retention metrics regardless of the current size of your agency.

Retention starts at the beginning, during the selection process

As with many parts of our business, taking good notes is essential. When a candidate is in the selection process, there are clues to their motivations, fears, strengths, and weaknesses. Often we use the steps of the selection process to "deselect" or to focus on success factors in the first months being in the business. But in the timeline of a potential 20-plus-year career we are only using the vast amount of information we have for the first few steps of a marathon.

Aptitude tests, application forms, top 100 market booklets, candidate/ spouse interviews, and character references will tell us who this person is, why are they looking for a career change, and what fuel feeds their fires. Look not only with your recruiting glasses on but your retention ones too.

While we may be satisfied simply to have a qualified candidate in front of us, it's important to remain vigilant; we are the guardians of both doors into our agency: the front and the back.

Probe specifically on reasons why they are leaving their current job and sitting across the table from you now. Obviously, it's a significant deal breaker. Take the opportunity to learn how to not fall into the same trap. Ask, "If you're successful in being selected to our firm but not here two years from now, why do you think that would be?" Often they will tell you about their Achilles heel and deal-breakers that could happen.

Discuss their short-term and long-term goals to see if it aligns with what you're willing to offer. Perhaps they see your agency as a springboard because they hear you have great training, maybe their personal situation is fragile, or they prefer part-time work, and so on.

While you are trying to determine what makes the candidate tick, give them insight into what makes you and your agency tick too. Is what the candidate stands for aligned with what your agency stands for? Any significant dissociation here can lead to future friction or a loss of connection between the candidate and you. They can learn about you through your manager biography and your agency's story. If you don't have these then I strongly suggest you do, it is one of the most important pieces to separate your recruiting efforts from the other recruiter's.

Motivators that drive agents to join you can drive them away from you too

If the candidate is at your interviewing table now, they are still looking to satisfy something. Knowing what drives the person in the chair in front of you and matching that with the opportunities within your agency is paramount. Document these motivators and refer to them often in your follow-up meetings with the candidate throughout the selection process and the agent throughout their career. At the end of the day, the root of motivation is often CONTROL. It's the reason many of us have become self-employed, right? Here are some things I've heard candidates frustrated to control in their current jobs say they want:

- Ownership of their annual income and increases, no maximums or glass ceilings, stability over the long term, and growth of business equity
- Career security, they can't be downsized and our industry is largely recession-proof. When it's conservative we do more risk protection sales and when markets are booming we do more wealth products sales.
- Have work/life balance, vacations, being there for their kid's baseball games, and going to the gym
- Control of success they experience and not depending on a team member's work to be recognized. Our industry tends to recognize loudly and in diverse ways.
- Control of the mountains they can climb, and they can build the team around them to win
- They can decide what skills to become proficient in, when and how to build their business as they see fit.

So I did some digging and looking at over 10 years of self-declared reasons for losing agents, common themes appeared. I hope you notice that underwriting is not on the list below.

So what are factors we can affect? From analyzing records of over 50 terminations in our agency, I found we could have affected about 70 percent of these terminations. This is where we changed our approach and now have quadrupled the retention numbers seen elsewhere.

- 25 percent – not developing viable markets, insufficient sales activity, and production results
- 20 percent – failed to understand how to leverage the compensation model to obtain desired income, managing business expenses and fluctuating commissions
- 10 percent –the Agency doesn't "care" anymore, which usually means connection and recognition isn't how they want it to be
- 10 percent –someone in their support circle is eroding their enthusiasm for what they do, or who they are doing it with. This is often spouse, parent, friends, or mentor you did not assign.
- 5 percent – lack of professional development in areas that mattered to them.

Some factors we CANNOT influence once contracted are:

- 10 percent – quality of advisor. Sometimes we find out quickly they were just a poor hire and not a good fit to the role despite our selection process. These agents should be let go sooner rather than later as they can lower the overall quality of your agency.
- 10 percent – outside opportunity. Perhaps there was an available block of business that is outside your firm, or their spouse gets job in another city, or another recruiter is "actively" pursuing them.
- 5 percent – The agent quits the reporting manager, but don't actually quit the career. We can all think of someone who has said "I like the career and I love the company but I just can't stand the manager here!"
- 5 percent – The great unknown. Sometimes you just get a resignation letter under your door Monday morning after the agent has spent the weekend packing up their office. We may never truly know what happened to make them leave.

Looking at why agents are leaving I have found that increased mentoring and joint fieldwork, greater access to development opportunities, addressing compensation issues before they happen, increased communication and recognition tactics targeted to groups of agent, as well as the conscientious inclusion of an agent's support circle can greatly impact retention numbers.

Does compensation affect behavior?

Why do clients stay with certain advisors and not with others? Clients see value in keeping good business relationships with agents that they trust to guide them. The same is true between agencies and advisors; they will stay with you if they see value in doing so.

Successful advisors know that it's more profitable and sustainable to keep existing clients on their books instead of replacing them every year. The same can be said for agencies keeping agents rather than rotating them. GAMA Foundation says we spend $150,000-$250,000 in first year of a recruit's career. Many companies have an assortment of production bonuses, recruiting bonuses, anniversary bonuses, co-op budgets for marketing and advertising, base incomes in the first year, training budgets, and so on.

There is a huge influx of resources and money at the beginning of their careers but where are the budgets and bonuses for 4th year retention? Luckily, you don't need a lot of money to effectively retain agents. So what can you do to keep them with you?

Establish a Retention Officer

It's remarkable; our industry commonly has dedicated roles for office managers, technology support, training managers, administrators, marketing directors, compliance officers, branch managers, and certainly recruiters. However, in my research of the topic I have rarely seen someone dedicated in keeping agents that keep our agencies running. Why is that?

The first step to positively affect retention is having someone accountable for it. Whether an additional hat for someone on your team or a dedicated position will depend on two things:

1. how big of a retention problem you believe you have
2. how much you want to impact the problem

This manager will be responsible for retention metrics as part of their quarterly or annual business plans. Give the Retention Officer (RO) the resources and power to do their job as they need to focus on the four "R's" of retention:

- Re-recruiting them using their career motivators
- Reminding them of the value proposition of your company
- Re-lighting enthusiasm for what they do
- Re-connecting agents to your organization, both mentally and geographically

What kind of manager makes a good RO? This person needs to be good at joint fieldwork, understands compensation and recognition systems flawlessly, is approachable, and infectiously enthusiastic about your agency. There is a wide audience from wandering rookies to grumpy senior agents that should be comfortable with this person.

One of the best ways for your agency to identify trends and reasons why agents are leaving your organization is to have the Retention Officer conduct all termination interviews. An objective "out" interview is an opportunity for closure for both the candidate and the agency, and it tells you why people are leaving. They may not tell the branch or recruiting manager the complete truth due to embarrassment, but they may tell the RO. From this evidence, you can make changes to mitigate the problem. For example, if your RO tells you four of the last six agents who left your agency did so because of the lure of a competitor's commission structure then perhaps it's time to run a compensation clinic for your rookies!

Segmenting agents to be more effective in retention

You only have so much time and energy for running your business every day. It can be more efficient to exert effort on groups rather than individual agents. We know this strategy when training agents so why not apply the same approach for retaining them?

Sales professionals regularly divide and categorize masses of clients, centres of influence, and prospects. It's efficient, fair, and a proven way to work with large numbers of clients. A bronze client gets an annual review and a return call within 48 hours, whereas a gold client gets an annual review, 24-hour call backs, quarterly statements, written financial summaries, and a bottle of wine on their birthday. Let's use the same methods when dealing with agents working with us. Some categories we can begin using immediately because virtually all of us have these groups of agents walking our halls. Depending on your organization's product line and business models, you may want to adapt these categories to maximize its effect.

- Experienced agent: over five years in the business either inside or outside of your agency
- Junior agents: under five years in the business
- Special groups: such as women's and ethnic markets, or even clusters of agents far away from you
- Generational groups: such as baby boomers, Generation X and Y
- Production level: a natural category to start with as we want to keep our top performers but remember to apply strategies focussed on tenure and psychological traits too
- Manager candidates: agents demonstrating leadership DNA can have special attention paid to them for opportunities and support to foster success their current agent role as well as develop future management potential. Remember, if you see potential in them, chances are others both inside and outside your company do as well.

- <u>Succession Planning:</u> identified agents that need a successor in next 1-3 years can be focussed on. It can be part of their business plan or something you watch due to their age or health concerns.

Street-Proof Your Agents

Rear-view tracking and reporting of your agency retention is not sufficient. You can be proactive in keeping agents safe when out in the world. Just like a parent; by addressing potential issues and influences before they happen you are forearming them. Tell them what's out there, as we can't be around to guide them every moment of every day. Instead of a stranger with candy it's a rival company trying to attract your agents away!

Retention planning is long term, not an overnight fix. Monitor any changes like a new competitor in town or concerning trends you observe in your area of responsibility and connect to susceptible agents quickly. When approach letters and emails start coming to your agents it is a good time to let agents know that if they haven't been contacted they will and if they have questions or concerns to come and speak to you directly. Better yet, set up a time to discuss that specific company and how it works.

When street proofing your agents connection to them is key and include their spouse and even community in this equation too. Conversations are more effective if they are comfortable talking to you. Being proactive now equals less crisis control later. Before we put our retention strategies in place we had a bad seed leave and take four agents with them. Several years later a similar situation happened but no one moved an inch because they were clear on the value of being with our agency. While you may see them one hour a day for coaching that also means they have twenty-three hours left in that day for internal and external influences to affect them. Street proofing means your message stays with them even when you physically can't be there.

Compensation and Communication

Eliminate ANY confusion on how they get paid and how your competitor's pay. No matter how good you are at this, be better! Compensation clinics, invite successful peers to assist, show that longer careers equal greater equity and stability are some of the strategies. Discuss and train diverse income streams; teach every way they can make money, even if not in your company's product line such as disability insurance, group benefits providers, traveller's insurance, and health and dental companies, as well as children's scholarship franchises. Show competitor compensation too, especially those nearby, be fair. Let them hear it from you, and not that kid on the playground. Don't be scared to do this!

In succession planning clinics, use case studies from your agency and even have these agents come in to facilitate the workshop. Discuss in detail how blocks of business can be passed on, and the importance of finding a successor they want to take over their business. We are on the doorstep of a time where companies that understand and facilitate succession planning will have a competitive edge in a shrinking workforce.

If your organization has retirement package for agents in your model then ensure they completely understand how it works as they get close to vesting. If you have Defined Contribution plans or stock matching then show them advantages when they maximize it through clinics designed to discuss increasing agent's net worth, and at these sessions discuss long-term goals for the value they would like to achieve before transitioning their block of business.

Create mid-year statements (see example in previous section) and remember to speak at a 12-year-old level, use graphics and avoid jargon because the spouses will read it. Subjects that have generated interest in the past are five-year income tracking (graphs are great visuals), residual income from as many sources as you can identify, assets under management (AUM) built. If appropriate illustrate the "mortgage" payment schedule of any blocks of business they have purchased, demonstrate the growth of their retirement package and business equity, recognize bonuses and designations earned as well as the campaigns and conventions qualified. Lastly, describe future opportunities this year to leverage any company programs to increase an agent's net worth.

If you take a genuine interest in their accomplishments, they will appreciate it. We are all pretty good at this, but the RO can expand on what you're currently doing. Show past accomplishments and new mountains to climb, leverage what they respond to whether fun experiences, personalized gifts, or paying for licenses/designations, and don't forget to promote, pump, and praise to the right person. It may not be the advisor; it could be their spouse, parent, or even the person who referred them into the business. Discover who that influential person is at their annual planning reviews if you didn't during the selection process.

Recognition and Development – Always have something going on at your agency

Offer specialized training for different groups, and facilitate classes for designations and additional licenses, give gift cards towards the costs of these classes. Make your strong agents stronger. Create a 48-week training program taking time away for last two weeks of the year for holidays and the first two weeks of year for AGMs and start-ups. Invite pre-contract recruits, the agent's assistants, and potential successors too. On top of regular training and branch events that need to happen in your agency, you can run each of these sessions four times a year.

1. Compensation clinics, talk about different streams of incomes, and competitors too
2. Wealth workshops taught by top wealth performers in your agency
3. Living benefits clinics such as disability, long term care, and critical illness
4. Succession planning workshops co-presented by recent agents who have been through it
5. Premium Club, talk about large insurance cases over $5,000 annual premium

6. Needs Analysis tools and software
7. Health clinics, demonstrate methods and sales strategies to have a well-rounded practise
8. Group Benefits, rotate providers your agents use regularly
9. Technology lunch-and-learns with assistants, learn how to use it to leverage time effectively
10. Convention Club luncheons held quarterly with those tracking to qualify
11. Introduction to Management Day, always build your bench strength
12. Assistant training sessions

The Retention Formula

In this next section, we will apply a simple formula that can aid in how you develop your own retention strategies in your agency.

PSYCHOLOGY + COMMUNICATION STYLE = RETENTION

We will review the traits and psychologies of common groups of agents and discuss how to adapt methods of communication that the group readily accepts and can be effective in staying connected to them. The sum of these two values has led to our agency retaining good agents while leveraging time and effort.

Retaining Baby Boomer Agents

These are the agents entering retirement age in the next 10 to 15 years. They are born between 1946 and 1964 and they represent almost half of the current workforce at 80 million strong. Boomers can't be retained forever but with no "career expiration date," they may stick around in our industry longer than peers in other occupations. Originally, we thought this group would be the hardest to retain, and they ended up being the easiest.

Traits & Characteristics of Baby Boomers

The baby boomers have a strong work ethic, and want to make a difference in their careers with successful organizations. They are competitive and driven due to largest birth year experienced; remember this group had to compete to get a spot on their local sports teams. These individuals pay attention to traditional career advancement, recognition, and titles both inside and outside company. They plan to stay with their employer over longer periods of time, unless you give them a reason to leave.

How to Communicate to Boomers

They readily accept phone calls and face-to-face meetings as the best connection; they want to look you in the eye. Involve spouses and VIPs in career wins and milestones and they are the last holdouts who appreciate framed letters and certificates for their achievements.

How to Retain Boomers

Understand their evolving work/life balance as their work is no longer the top priority, living well is. Remind them they "make a difference" to the agency and clients, they want meaningful work. Involve them in the agency's direction and vision. When implementing change in the environment, ask them for feedback as a respected individual. Make them part of building the office, have some of them as the final interview step; they want to take some ownership of good agents in the office too.

Retaining Generation X Agents

This group of 40-somethings were born between 1965 and 1980, are 46 million strong, and represent approximately 40 percent of the workforce today.

Traits & Characteristics of Gen X Agents

This group is skeptical of messages they hear because in their life very little is permanent. They grew up where family divorce rates exploded, saw both parents working, moved up the corporate ladder, and got laid off anyway. They prefer informal relationships in the workplace and with authority. Like the boomers, they value work/life balance. They are mobile for careers if they need to be and want to be stimulated in their workplace. They expect to have opportunities for increased business growth, through succession plan and blocks of business coming available. Lastly, they learn quickly, often on their own, and are technologically advanced.

How to Communicate to Gen X

Reinforce they are supported with professionals who can teach them what they need to be successful. This group needs to hear the truth. They question everything and will know if you don't know the answer. Phone, text, and impactful emails work best with this group.

Generation X won't respect you just because you're a manager, in fact they will challenge you with questions because of your position. A great analogy when comparing Boomers to Gen Xers is when approaching a black belt karate master. A baby boomer will respect the person first and unless proven otherwise will continue to respect their shown position. A Gen X will throw a punch at the karate master first to see if the person is worth respecting.

How to Retain Gen X

Allow them to work independently, within compliance standards of course, to control their business. Be upfront, clear, and fact-based with your communications. Remember they want the truth so eliminate frustrating bureaucracies to give clear access to information and make decisions pertinent to their practise quickly. Have FUN and give them reasons to brag to their peers about what their company did last week. Sell the value of your agency training to become the professionals they originally joined you to be.

Live life with excitement, creating campaign incentives based on cool experiences will get their attention. Ideas like awarding swords for sales campaigns, trips in hot air balloons, and shooting at rifle ranges for convention qualifiers has been highly appreciated by this group. This group desires bigger and better offices to show their progress in their careers, these things may not matter to everyone at your agency but it matters to this group.

Retaining Generation Y Agents

This newest workforce cohort was born after 1980 and represents 20 percent of the workforce currently, but with 80 million strong and not all are in the workforce yet, it's predicted they will be 75 percent of the total working population by year 2025. This is the hardest group to retain, but perhaps it's because they are the hardest to keep their attention!

Traits and Characteristics of Gen Y

Focused on the family and friends, they are outspoken and speak their minds without reservation. They have a global (diverse) view of the world because they have constant access to it. You will find this cohort pursues self-improvement at a relentless pace of what they think important, not necessarily what you think they should be learning at the moment. They can take, absorb and communicate information at the same time which is great for them, but dizzying to most of us. When dealing with money they often earn to enjoy life. Lastly, this group wants to be treated with respect and work with bright, creative individuals so making a study group can show appeal when training them.

How to Communicate to Gen Y

Two words: immediate feedback. Texting after every sale is appreciated and will come to be expected! Let them know that their viewpoint is respected and valued. They want to be involved in all discussions. Remember that their parents asked this generation where they wanted to go for family vacations for Pete's sake!

If you want them to be part of agency events and sales campaigns then include representative from this group as part of planning them. It has been my experience they can generate awesome campaign ideas, which will actually motivate this group. A small caveat here; expect their ideas to be a bit "out of the box" and may not appeal to all the agents you have. Establish mentor programs with competent and respected agents, they are particularly drawn to protégé relationships

How to Retain Gen Y

One of the best strategies I've seen work is having a manager dedicated to this group that understands their world and is likely a Gen Y themselves. This group has a "pack mentality" meaning they stick with their friends. This can be advantageous as a good source of recruiting as they like working with their friends. The flip side of this is they can also leave together arm-in-arm to a competitor and see no harm in doing it.

Provide them with a very strong role model; dress and act like you want them to be. Immediately when contracted, it's a good idea to orient them to the agency's vision. Be super flexible when training and coaching: offer training courses online and either FaceTime or Skype coaching calls. Some of my best coaching sessions with Gen Y agents have been using a video conference via their smartphones while they were driving or waiting for a client to show up. Continually discuss career progression and their "next step" within the organization

Spouse and VIP's as Agency Connectors

One of the best things we've done in the last seven years to affect retention is have the spouses be agency advocates. When recruiting candidates in the selection process or at annual business reviews talk to them about the importance of involving their VIP. Get permission to correspond to their home by letter or email so as to keep their family informed of their achievements.

If the candidate is married, you have to recruit and retain two people into your agency, not just one. It's important to send thank you cards to spouses after big accomplishments and include children's names too; they had to sacrifice time with the agent while they were doing sales appointments five nights a week.

A great idea I adopted years ago was to have the spouse and children's names in my smartphone contact title. It's easy to do and the benefits are fantastic! When the agent calls you for something, you will see all their family names flash on the screen to remind you to include them in your conversation. When the business at hand is dealt with, make sure you enquire about their family and take a genuine interest in it. These conversations leave an indelible impression and makes the connection between you and your agents that much stronger.

Annual recognition lunch with spouses /VIPs

Use an agenda or template similar to the mid-year letter to visually show income history, blocks of business metrics, growth of their client block, and so on. Talk about recent accomplishments in front of them and brag about their partner. Agents will often downplay their wins when they get home, you can compensate for that at this meeting. Discuss year-to-date tracking of what they wanted to accomplish as well as any "stretch goals" and what is needed to achieve them. Lastly, talk about the next natural step in their business; plant the seeds while the partner is listening.

The Retention Officer can oversee a calendar of fun social events allowing advisors and their families to bond in a non-work environment. During recognition dinner events offer to have the agent and their spouse come to collect the prize together at the front of the room. Even at in-house agency presentations you can show images of the agent and their spouse for all acknowledgments. These photos are easy to get; just take the couple's pictures at agency social events and even their Facebook page. I have found that the significant others are great ambassadors of the agency and can be part of a winning retention strategy.

Retaining Senior Agents

Remember this is not the same as someone who is chronologically older or from a prior generation. You can have a "senior agent" who is a 35-year-old Gen Y but has been with your agency for seven years. These veteran advisors often get overlooked at times because they now run a steady business practise and don't knock on your door for help much anymore. The things that helped them survive and thrive in the first five years may not be sufficient to launch the next five years. Motivators change after the "dangerous adolescence" as income is more stable, the threat of failing diminishes, and there is less attraction to shiny prizes.

They key now is to appreciate them and remind them of what they have built with their hard work. Respect their experience when dealing with them. You can be informal at times and spur of the moment visits to say "good work" are sometimes as important as recognition plaques. Breakfasts, lunches, and quick coffee meetings with no defined agenda are fun and spontaneous. If you're in the area where their office is and have some time, make a point to pop by or at least leave them a note.

Connection is more important than coaching at this stage of their career but leverage additional resources your company has to offer to make them even better. They may have been too busy "surviving" the early years to learn everything that is available like personal retirement and business planning, large case specialists, and even additional funds from HO to augment their current business practises such as client appreciation events.

Ask for their Influence

Make them part of the Board of Directors at your agency, and if you don't have one ask them to help create one! Establish standards for qualifying for your office's mentor program. Have them help recognize junior agents at Gala dinners as presenters. Sometimes it can mean far more to a rookie agent getting a trophy from them than you. Make senior agents part of the recruiting process as a final "sign off" of recruits coming to the agency.

Lastly, you can create an internal speakers bureau on key areas they are great at. Then promote them internally for your own events and to other agencies in your company as experts in their field. Remove obstacles and distractions from their path so they can keep working, they can deal with the little stuff now.

Junior agents

Somewhere in the first five years they will have an identity crisis. They may have felt they were pretending being an agent the first year or fighting to survive the second and third years, but one day they will catch themselves in the mirror and think "Is this who I will be forever?" Peer-to-peer accountability or mentorship is often stronger than anything managers can apply.

CAUTION: If you don't supply a mentor, it may happen anyway and that's not always a good thing; sometimes under-performing or miserable agents enjoy company with those having a bad day or a competitor who smells an opportunity to "coach" your agent. We can all probably think of a disastrous self-appointed mentor that was fatal to a rookie's success.

Constantly refine annual and quarterly plans on their goals and dreams.

These are the magnets that will pull them through the tough days. Recognize them against their own peer group. They can't compete against established senior agents, and this can be discouraging. Focus on criteria for recruit of the year or advisor of the month. Often they need carrots to get from one month to the next, or even one week to the next. It can be tangible such cufflinks, gift cards, or a suit or intangible like time with you. It may sound hard to believe but one of the most rewarding things I've done is when I spent an overnight business trip with one of my agents. We visited a distant city to meet with his COIs. Years afterwards, we still recollect that weekend where we both learned a great deal about one another's lives and became good friends. Like a parent, some kids would gladly trade a bought gift for some exclusive time with. Try it.

Special Groups to Pay Special Attention to

Ethnic Groups

At my branch, we have large Chinese, Filipino, and Punjabi communities in our area of responsibility. We try to recognize and support events for these markets. I believe it is important to show an effort to be involved in the community your advisors work within. Learn a bit of their language, it really goes a long way. A great book to have in your office, and should certainly be on the desk of the RO, is Kiss, Bow, and Shake Hands as it covers virtually every culture you will likely recruit or have in your halls. It discusses basic customs for greeting and working with agents and clients with ethnic backgrounds.

Additionally, you can end congratulations via text in their language; it's easy, just type into Google Translate the message you want to convey and then copy and paste it to an email or text message to the agent. The RO can create an agency calendar to mark special dates for different cultures in your agency. You can even host training and special presentations in their language as well as have special cuisines as the menu items for these workshops.

Gender Groups

As an industry, we lose more women than men proportionately as agents; and we lose far more in the first two years of the career. Pay particular attention to this group, and the best way to know what they would appreciate is to ask, not assume. They sometimes want to hear from successful women from similar backgrounds as them. We have run "Wine, Women and Wealth" workshops for the agents and their female clients. These have been incredibly successful when we host female presenters from a wide range of professions as speakers.

Geographically Separated Groups

Half of my agents are outside of my agency walls. They have set up clusters of multi-agent locations within 30 km of my central agency. These satellite offices that are farther away need to feel connected to our home branch so setting up Skype calls or video webinars for training where needed is a good idea. Proactively send materials directly to them (versus them having to wait to pick it up once a week) or better yet drop it off during a visit. Why not host special guest speakers and even have sales campaign launches at their location? Make sure others in your agency know where they are "on the map" and keep this group connected to you.

Retaining your Management Team

Do not overlook your agency's "sales force" either as your managers are just as entrepreneurial as your agents. They have similar motivational engines as agents so the tenure and generational strategies we've covered in this section are just as valid. Avoid the mistake of assuming that because of their titles on their business cards they are a homogenous group, they are not!

Keep in mind the importance of "wins"; agents can get 8-12 sales or wins per month, managers may only get a handful per year if their only focus is recruiting new agents. This can lead to frustration and leaving the role or your agency. If you have a significant numbers of managers in your agency, you can construct Manager Cup competitions (perhaps the winner goes with you to LAMP) based on relevant performance criteria. Award this trophy at the annual recognition event just as you do with agents.

You can also create monthly challenges and incentives during sales campaigns for agents, possibly based on numbers of agent qualifiers they work with to achieve it as well. Rotate managers in agency development plans and specific tasks to keep them engaged and cross-trained.

If you are leading the agency and it comes to your manager's individual career plans, do they actually know how to be better managers? Are you coaching towards achieving their goals or simply meeting them weekly to tell them what you need them to accomplish next week month? Do they feel you supporting them and are you showing value? Are you grooming your own successor or a competent second-in-charge? Answer these questions and see if you can alter your own way of thinking, it could reap dividends for your agency, as well as them.

Always lead by example! Credibility leads to value learning from you and you want them to feel they can learn around you. Role model what they can aspire to be, be impeccable in your dress and deportment.

Recruiting and Retention Tree

I find this to be a great visual tool and your RO can create and update these diagrams to help you with your quarterly and annual conversations with your managers. It shows a bigger perspective of their recruiting impact to the agency and the retention trends by manager and NOT just by the entire agency. By looking at retention as an agency aggregate, you may fail to be aware of a manager who is really growing your agency versus bringing lots of recruits in only to lose them in year two. Check out whether these agents who left are still in the industry. This asks the question: Is my sales manager recruiting for my agency, or the competition's organization?

You can build a recruiting and retention tree like this for your entire agency to identify if agents are leaving you or the industry. Go back 10 years if you want and map your manager's recruiting legacy.

Managers are future-looking as a mindset largely paying attention to their targets for the month or the quarter and we are optimistic by nature. We face forward to what we are building now, it is both a strength and a weakness for managers. This diagram can illustrate long-term trends (both good and bad) and we should learn from what we've built in the past to get even better in the future.

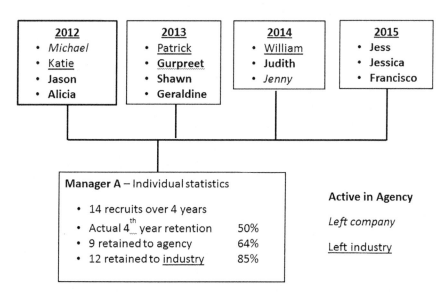

Make the people in your agency Sticky

In conclusion, not paying close attention to retention has been a luxury of a large workforce pool to select from. The next ten or so years as the boomers enter full retirement we will need to retain as many agents and managers as possible for not only succession planning but to also pass on experience and service a massive client block who may live another thirty years.

We won't have the luxury to ignore retention when we lose a third of the agency talent needed to keep our organization thriving. Count the number of 55-plus agents in your halls and tell me you aren't just a little bit concerned.

An advisor you don't lose is one you don't have to replace; never forget that retention is the other side of the growth coin. Anything you can do to show value to your advisors will make them "sticky" to your organization. If they are active, appreciated, and connected to your agency, they will likely stay with you.

Re-recruiting Agents Throughout their Careers

It is particularly important to re-recruit agents around the two or three year benchmark; it's the dangerous "adolescence" period of the career. At this time they are either struggling in the career and very much open to anything that could potentially save them, or they think they have kind of figured it out and perhaps feel they have outgrown what your agency can offer. This is the dangerous period where agents are the most susceptive to outside forces to either leave or change companies. Senior agents have survived this period and are largely "sticky" in the career now.

"If the grass seems greener on the other side of the fence, they probably have a higher water bill"; meaning that moving over to the other side of the fence in pursuit of a more perfect situation will likely have very real costs to it. Costs such as losing part of your client block in the transition, disconnecting from the resources and people who have been part of building your business, and the strains of rebuilding in a new corporate culture.

At the end of the day, most of the big financial organizations in our country are very similar to one another. It's a level playing field for the most part: with small variations, the insurance product line and pricing is the same, the caliber of training and support is the same, access to investments, underwriting, and so on.

Why an agent joins your branch over another branch in their community is because of the recruiting manager they are speaking to. From this person they can have a feel of "fit" to the industry and culture. They are also always judging if they truly believe the management of the agency will help them be successful. So if an agent is now "disturbable" it can be because they have lost connection to the coaching manager or they're simply not getting what they need from your organization. The agent might totally be competent to sell insurance, group benefits, and investments now thanks to your assistance but now something else is missing.

Remember you were able to recruit them from their former career because they felt they weren't getting what they wanted from it. Now that they are in the financial industry doesn't make them immune for someone new, either inside or outside our industry, to recruit them away again. All professional recruiters from every industry are well trained in finding that loose thread and pick at it.

You would think that we as sales managers would understand this better; we aren't the only ones who think the agent is valuable. If you want to keep your people, after you have asked them to leave their last employer for greener pastures with you, then street-proof them before the next recruiter takes them to lunch to talk about what their grassy meadow has for them.

Parents street-proof their children to not get into a stranger's car, not walk down dark streets alone, and to stand up to bullies in the playground. Sales managers are like the parents of the agency, it is their responsibility to protect and educate your advisors about what they will encounter in the real world when we're not around to guide them. They will be approached by many sources that will try to pull them off the path. Hope and denial won't work here; it's not about "if," it's about "when." They will be approached by several organizations every week, every month, every year. This constant bombardment that people find them desirable might be very flattering. Likely the agent is perfectly happy today but there may be a day when they are not, whether after a declined large premium case or they weren't accepted into a management program. Situations like this happen every day. But this time when they pick up the phone with a recruiter on the other side of the line saying, "Hey, let's get together for some coffee," they might just go meet with them.

Part of your retention strategy needs to be reasserting the value your organization brings, especially the parts they were attracted to in the first place like business marketing support or your retirement packages. Repeatedly emphasizing the strengths of your compensation model, along with timelines and realistic income projections, should be a part of regular training too. Lastly, education of the different agency structures and their compensation models should be discussed. Be fair and objective when you present this, they will smell it if you're being biased.

Compensation should be part of the training syllabus of advisors in the first two years. For example, I like to run compensation clinics at least two times a year covering anything to do with how they get paid (taking over blocks of business, creating multiple lines of residual incomes, how to leverage our stock matching programs, incorporating their business, etc.). These boardroom events are usually wall to wall with agents from a range of tenures and most come multiple times over the years because as their business develops so will their interest in certain facets of compensation.

By constantly reminding them of what they currently have in their hands as well as providing a heads-up to what they will encounter "out there" will allow them to avoid those situations and tell the recruiter at the end of the phone, "Thank you but I'm not interested." Or if they do meet with them they at least will understand what they're hearing, ask educated questions, and not be bamboozled, and lastly be able to make a proper appraisal of what may be a potential opportunity versus the opportunity they're currently sitting in.

At the end of the day, and I said this at the beginning, the financial industry need good people to be able to help protect people and build wealth in our country. Obviously, you need good people in your branch too, but advisor movement to some degree is inevitable. However, if you feel too many agents are leaving your branch then look deeper within the organization to identify and address contributing factors. I believe that in many, not all, situations the agent was probably in the best place initially, but they either lost sight of that or someone didn't remind them enough.

A strategy for retention is setting up a schedule to connect with agents for timely education and key messages. It can be lunch on their birthday, providing a gift on their company anniversary, mail appreciation letters to their spouses thanking them for their support. Every year I do mid-year report cards for my "A" agents, which includes increases/decreases in income, numbers of clients with life and health products, wealth AUM, campaign performance, MDRT credits, etc. While you could do one for everyone in your organization, I find to do a good job is very time intensive unless you have a champion for it.

One of the most fun and powerful things I've done in recent years is taking successful rookie agents and their spouses/partners for a meal. At this time together I surprise them with a summary of all the accomplishments, income tracking, growth of their retirement packages, reachable year-end goals, their potential for management, and so on. Often the spouse is surprised and really proud of their partner, the agent may simply not be one to brag or get into details on what they have built so far. This is a chance to review recent accomplishments as well as short, mid, and long-term goals the agent is on track to achieve.

A significant part of a good retention strategy is to include their spouses, or someone who they feel is an important part of their lives such as a parent or mentor. Where possible, include these people in agency social events, annual campaign getaways, year-end gala recognition dinners, and so on. If there's a weekend celebration, find ways to include the spouses in daily activities, or even take key couples for lunches or interesting excursions. Most people want to see their partner do well; they want glimpses into the world that takes so much of their partner's time. It's also important for them to connect with other spouses and see they are not alone and that the industry is filled with good people.

Of course, this is not only important from a culture-building perspective but these VIPs are with them when you're not around, like after coming back after a long night with a difficult client. A "connected" spouse can stop an advisor from making hasty decisions or leaving the organization more effectively than likely you can. In the heat of the moment, or in the immediate aftermath of a really bad day, their partner will remind them of all the reasons why they joined the career, why they chose your company, and how happy they have been in the past. I've seen some spouses actually call the sales manager directly to help their partner get back on track. Nurture and develop these alliances, and don't underestimate their influence, for or against.

The Retention Officer can create an annual schedule of key opportunities for identified at-risk agents to be a part of a strategy or even a "global" retention plan for your office. At one-on-one meetings, these ROs can reaffirm the advisor's reasons for becoming an agent with your company. Look inside their agent files for declared goals and dreams when they started, what they wanted to accomplish, and perhaps the reason why they left their former employer (providing you actually took notes on this topic during their selection process). Are these motivators being addressed currently?

You may not be able to hire a specific person for this role, and perhaps you don't have to. Unless a wholesale change is needed, you can probably identify a current manager who has the personality and skill-set to perform this role. In exchange for taking on this additional responsibility, you could lighten their load in terms of recruiting targets. After all, if they can demonstrably help the branch keep more people you don't have to replace they are, in fact, helping the branch grow. It may not be pure recruiting, but keeping the recruits brought in can be considered the other side of the recruiting coin.

The RO can get started building an agent profile worksheet to learn more about the agent. These documents can certainly have their performance records included but it's more important to add information about them such as hobbies, spouse and kids names, vacations they are planning, ethnic festival that apply to them, and so on. Once the plan is in place set a monthly or quarterly schedule to meet with these advisors to reinforce and support "hot buttons." Putting regular entries in the ROs calendar will make it easier for them to stick with it.

If you do not have a retention strategy, sometimes you won't know there is a problem until you see people leave. Instead of managing the situation, you will be doing damage control: re-recruiting the agent back, talking to other potential "infected" advisors, and so on. It's far easier to keep the ball rolling on a well thought-out strategy than dealing with it when there is trouble.

You won't change your head office paradigms when it comes to a retention philosophy, but if it's important to the health and growth of your local business then you can make changes; it's within your control.

Do You Know Your ABC's?

Alex Chan

Over the years, not only while working as a financial advisor since 1987 but also as a sales manager, we have made recommendations to our agents to classify their blocks of business into various categories such as A, B, or C. Some advisors have even gone a step further using A, B, C+, C, D, and E to designate clients. One may ask why this practise has become mainstream in the financial advising community. It all comes down to the service offering we provide to our clients based on a time and revenue formula, along with more personal criteria based on what the agent's business and goals are, referred to as the key differentiators for each client segment.

In the early days, we all fell into the trap of saying to our clients, "It doesn't matter if you are a big or small client to me, I will treat you the same and be there for you 24/7." Well today that just cannot be the case anymore especially when seasoned advisors may have a client base over 1,000. Some advisors may even have the odd C or D client that has large policies and wealth assets with them but they are not an A or B segment. There is only so much time during our workweek to equalize the classic work, family, personal, health, lifestyle balance.

Currently, as a sales manager, this "segmentation" is becoming more prevalent in the independent Managing General Agency businesses. As a leading national MGA, it is virtually impossible and completely uneconomical to offer our complete suite of products, services, and support to every single advisor associated with us.

We have adopted classifications for our advisors that can range from A to D. Not always is this segmentation based on volumes of business although it is certainly an important criteria. We apply such criteria as business volumes, ease of doing business with, high or low maintenance, great in compliance, "top quality and persistent business," or even "they like us and we like them" (sounds silly but true). We ask our sales managers in each office to use these classifications so that we can properly support these advisors with the appropriate package that they deserve and have achieved.

Top A+ and A advisors are awarded with such incentives as Regional and National Education Conferences which develop them and to thank them for their business. We also offer professional services such as our Underwriting Consultant, Business Succession Planning Specialist, VP Training and Development, and Tax and Estate Services to these top tier advisors.

The B and C+ advisors are also personally met with each quarter over lunch or dinner to discuss their business and assist in the areas that we identify so that we can provide them with exceptional services. We also discuss what it would take to move them up a category if they show interest in doing so. Our case managers can see the categories we designate so that A, B, and C+ advisors receive priority handling by them.

We have carefully tailored our agency value propositions to each category, as it is very similar to the business of an advisor. We find this fair and our advisors would tend to agree. It also provides our C+ and C advisors an incentive to achieve a higher behind the scenes status within our organization. Independent advisors like to talk about their business to their peers and brag about the recent conference they attended as an "A" agent or how great the quarterly dinner meeting was with the underwriter or fund manager.

Don't get me wrong, even our C-, D, and E advisors receive excellent support in the areas of education and training, technology, product shelf, compliance, case management, and in-force services so they are not neglected. From time to time, a C-, D, or E advisor who does not fit into our model has been asked to find another MGA catering more to their marketplace, performance, and style of business.

This "segmentation" has also found its way into the head offices of our industry as well as the marketing departments of our insurance and mutual fund companies. One company (that I will not name) has six classifications for internal use when dealing with advisors. A number of companies I know have other "behind the scenes" calculators to determine the levels of support the advisors receive.

Segmentation is not necessarily based on new or in force business, it also allows the Regional representative and VPs to provide feedback. An example I've seen from A to D from an insurance company starts at "A" as Core Supporter, "B" as Growth Supporter, "C+" as Contributor, "C" as New Supporter, "D" as Potential, and "E" as Fallen Angel. All are appropriate descriptions and each has its own level of support provided by the company. In some regions, company reps have over 3,000 contracted brokers to work with. They simply cannot be spinning their wheels consistently meeting, spending time, and money on their D and E agents.

There are always exceptions and the insurance and investment companies, financial advisors, and MGAs are sensitive to this. When looking at how they classify advisors, it very much falls into line of the seasoned financial advisor with a large clientele, the independent MGA, and of course the insurance and mutual fund companies. These companies have taken segmentation further and classify MGAs and Dealership accounts in a very similar fashion. In reality, this age-old process of client segmentation exists in almost every professional organization from banking, accounting, and legal so we are not applying this process in isolation. As a leading national Managing General Agency, we have found this to be an excellent model, which we apply to our independent advisors.

In our humble opinion, it makes great business sense and we are confident it will stand the test of time. It has garnered for us for the past two years in a row the Top Agency in Canada as reported by The Investment Executive.

By Alex Chan, CHS, CFP, CPCA, EPC, CFSB
Marketing Director BC
IDC Worldsource Insurance Network

'Snakes and Ladders' and other Gems

Robin J. Rankine

Managing and leading go hand in hand. This is a job of "doing" for sure but also requires us to think. Thinking followed by doing can make things change. We all know this, we need to learn and hone our craft through our own, and others, experiences. With this in mind, I have captured a small compilation of practises, ideas, or processes that have worked for me and our sales organization. Perhaps these can be helpful to you and your team as well.

Snakes and Ladders

This is mainly an internal thought process, a way of thinking that helps direct my actions. I have long used this term, "snakes and ladders," to describe the ups and downs of our business and more accurately what it takes to succeed. In particular, the art and science of agency building requires this philosophy of the children's game "Snakes and Ladders." You are moving along the game fine and your goal is in sight. Then you hit a "snake" and slide down, sometimes a long ways down. Or perhaps things are not going well in your agency but you keep doing the right things and then a ladder appears and you jump ahead of the pack.

As long as you apply, as the Kinder Brother's say "honest intelligent effort," there is only one way to lose and that is to stop rolling the dice. It really is an exercise in persevering. Keep doing the right things regardless of how good or bad things are going currently and you will get the outcome you desire. It's only a matter of time; you will move from where you are to where you want to be.

One "Wild Card" Call Daily

A simple and private idea I use and some of you likely use in different forms. I came across this idea 25 years ago and it still works well today. It goes like this: in sales there is always someone you should call as a prospective client but you don't have the courage or confidence today for some reason. Maybe your perception of their client profile intimidates you or you are not sure what to say. For whatever reason you don't call. As managers, we likely all have agent candidates that fit this category too. It happens to all of us once in a while.

The "Wild Card" Call idea is that once a day, just before you call it quits and go home, you make one more call to that client or candidate. Create that little extra blast of courage, confidence, and effort. What do you have to lose? Nothing, and there is a lot more to gain. This really works and results in some good things happening. Make it part of your daily routine and try it. Remember confidence is "memory of past successes" and this practise increases your odds of these wins occurring.

Recruiting Blitz Day

Once a week in our agency, it happens on Tuesdays, we kick our sales managers out of the office. That is to say, we want them out of the office all day doing what we call a "Recruiting Blitz Day." We have done this for about 15 years now and it works for us.

There are two recruiting goals for the day; one is activity based on what we call "Asks" and the other is results based which we call "Names." An "Ask" is asking someone to take a look at our career opportunity, or asking someone to refer us to someone who should. A "Name" is just that, the resulting potential candidate referrals or active personal observations of candidates from the day's activities. A superior "Blitz Day" would have 10 or more "asks" and 5 or more "names" coming from in-person active recruiting activities of the day. We record these and present the following morning in our weekly managers meeting as well as share some of the experiences surrounding our results.

Finding and Developing Managers

Finding: We prefer to "grow from within" a better method for our agency: investing the thinking and observation time into identifying agents in our organization that are consistently modelling the kinds of things we want. Do they have followers and do people come to them for advice and direction already? Then we carefully decide if it makes sense to offer them a chance to discover the manager opportunity and role. It does not have to be an automatic appointment to a management role and it is OK if they look at it but do not proceed. We obviously want people who want to do the role well.

On many occasions, we tried appointing managers from outside our organization and even from outside our industry: we have had temporary success but not sustainable success. I know it works for some agencies but in over 20 years of developing managers, not for us. The learning curve of licensing, training, product, technology, commissions, processes, compliance, and an array of other culture-specific competencies competes with the new manager's time. It seems to set a pattern of preoccupation with these things rather than the act of doing the recruiting job amongst other functions important to the agency.

Development: Amidst all other activities that vie for our time, I recommend the agency leader meets weekly with the new manager one-on-one each week for about an hour for at least the first two years in the role. Use a standing agenda or create one together to touch a variety of topics regularly and dig in on the critical ones. Create something of meaning like recruiting activity and their new advisor productivity, for the rookie manager to prepare ahead of time and bring with them.

Overall, we use a coaching and developing philosophy of "teach/coach/partner" with our advisors and this is very transferable to developing and working with managers too. Generally, we associate tenure with these categories: less than 2 years, 2 to 5 years, and 5-plus years in the business. With advisors, we use a weekly/monthly/quarterly review with their manager respectively for these three stages. For example, a new advisor meets and reviews with their manager on a weekly basis (teach group) for the first two years, then monthly (coach group) for years 2 through 5, and then quarterly (partner) thereafter.

For managers, when they are two years or less in the role we feel there is a lot of teaching and mentoring to occur. At a minimum, a lot of communication is needed between the agency head and the developing manager. So as with the developing advisor, the agency head meets weekly with the manager, progressing to monthly after 2 years in the role, and for a 5-year-plus managers we keep the pace of reviews monthly thereafter.

None of this scheduled review time structure in our coaching and development philosophy takes away from ad-hoc meetings or regular or spontaneous interactions between advisors and managers. It is simply scheduled "sacred time" for communication, reporting, supervision, development, and connection.

Building a Strong Culture

In reflecting on this topic, many thoughts come to mind. This is always a work in progress as you have to blend what is working with keeping things fresh. Remember the "snakes and ladders" analogy earlier. First and foremost, it starts with your expectations as the lead manager, not in isolation of the other team members but you are the gatekeeper to your culture. Good or bad, you have unique insights into the agency culture and are responsible for it. Ideally, your vision is to foster and grow a great "strong culture" that everyone will be proud of. To help elaborate on this thought I will share an example using our agency's mission and vision.

Mission: We are a professional, dynamic, profitable, growing financial centre. A team of passionate, diverse, professionals; making a meaningful difference in the lives of all our stakeholders.

Vision: To be the leader within the financial services industry and build to greatness through teamwork.

We have long used the term "Building to Greatness Through Team Work" in our quest to build a strong culture and become a strong financial services organization. We initially used this "slogan" over 20 years ago as a reoccurring sales campaign theme. It, along with the mission and vision, has taken on different forms and meaning over the years. However, it does help frame what it is we want to do and need to do, the culture we want to build and maintain, tweak and improve. Constantly referencing the "mission and vision" helps us in our decision making even at the micro level: from recruiting and selection to creating campaign rewards to local charity work.

"How we do things around here" is the best definition of culture I have heard of so far. This is particularly revealing of our agency culture and likely yours too. Sometimes we really like the answer this definition generates and other times we don't. We think about what we are building and can attribute the following components to a building strong culture as outlined in our mission and vision. Here a few examples of these components in action that have led to a consistently strong culture.

- Monday Morning Training Class
- Monday Night Phone Clinic and Phone Session (ran for last 15 years)
- Wednesday Morning Weekly Management Meeting (running for last 15 years)
- Company Sales Campaigns: Our agency staff, not the managers, takes a key leading role in designing the campaign promotion strategy and awards (for the last six years)
- Annual Christmas Party: A three-day mountain retreat involving advisor's families and support teams and has run for the last 13 years.
- Annual Awards Banquet: Every January for last 10 years with spouses and staff included
- Annual Reward Trip: We have run an out-of-country retreat for 15

years and it involves a brief business session and a lot of open agenda time with optional activities that foster lifelong relationships inside and outside of work.

- Summer BBQ: This is organized and hosted by the Advisor Association, as is the Annual Christmas Party, at the same location for 10 of the last 15 years.

Final Thoughts

In closing I hope you have gained at least one idea, process, or thought pattern that can complement your current model and drive greater success in your organization. I leave you with good wishes for your future success and a favourite quote in the words of former US President Abraham Lincoln, "I will study and prepare myself and one day my chance will come."

By Robin J. Rankine CLU, ChFC, CLU
Financial Centre Manager, Edmonton, Alberta
Sun Life Financial

Points to Remember from this Section

- Know the motivators why people join and leave you
- Establish a Retention Officer (RO)
- Retention formula for different cohorts of agents

Now add points you want to remember or refer back to

-
-
-
-

Notes:

_____

_____

_____

_____

_____

_____

_____

Section 5

What the Future May Hold

Client Block Size in the New Millennium

When you think about the future, the business practises of sales managers has gotten our industry this far but I doubt it will be sufficient to get our agencies where we need to be for the next 10, 20, or 30 years. Traditionally, eight hundred to a thousand clients have been a good block size for an agent. Often agents predominantly work within one product line whether life insurance, living benefits insurance, investments, fee for service planning, or a group benefit provider. Even if an agent is able with their agency to do more than one product line, they generally choose or naturally silo themselves into one of those categories.

With the demographic changes that lie ahead we will have less of us doing the work, but clients will still expect professional levels of service and will desire holistic agents that can answer a wide spectrum of questions and provide multiple solutions. We will be included in discussions in their workplace investment choices, personal insurances, possibly working alongside their accountants and lawyers to complete a "big picture" financial plan. We now work with peripheral partners that offer products and services we may not be able to do ourselves. While often only the top people diversified themselves in that way in the past, it will be the starting line of service in the future.

In my father's time, when he started the business, having a high school diploma (or sometimes not even that) along with an outgoing attitude was enough to start being an agent. In the 21st century, we are seeing the professional bar rise higher every year. Whether self-imposed by the individual, the agency, or industry regulators, I can see the day where dual-licensed Certified Financial Planners could be the new normal for entering our industry.

Leveraging Time – Technology and Assistants

Leveraging resources will be essential as we move forward in this new paradigm. We will have to stop agents driving all over a region in a given day; it is a drain of precious working hours. I personally drive 1,500 kilometres a week driving around to see my advisors and COIs. I bet advisors average 600 kilometres per week going to appointments. When client block size is substantially increased due to a shrinking workforce commuting like driving is unsustainable.

Instead, agents and managers will be able to offset this workload through additional manpower and technology support (and remember assistant support will be in higher demand too). I recommend to get an assistant as early as possible because it's better to outsource someone for $10 to $15 an hour to do the filing, confirming appointment, prepping quotes, following up with NSF payments, beneficiary change form, and so on. All of these activities are incredibly valuable to the running of a business but every precious "agent hour" will be focussed on servicing and growing business in the next evolution of the industry. The other leverage point is technology. Rather than commuting for an hour to meet clients, use videoconferencing tools like Skype or FaceTime to prepare or interview clients prior to the business transactions. You can send them documents to sign and send back. Be ruthless with your time. Make every minute useful and efficient.

One of the biggest reasons for leveraging technology or outsourcing administrative duties is simply compensation. An average client with a $100 a month premium on an insurance product can generate up to $1,500 in commissions for that agent. Now let us figure out what time was spent on completing that financial sale. Let's assume the agent had to meet with the client at least twice for one-hour meetings that each took one-hour roundtrip for commuting. That's four hours so far. Let's further assume it took an hour to prepare paperwork, generating quotes and comparisons. And another hour to drop off and review the policy so now up to about six hours. For padding let's put an hour and a half in there for follow-ups, rescheduling, or an extra meeting which gives us a grand total of 7 ½ hours required for this $1,500 commission.

You are getting paid about $200 an hour! This is equivalent to many downtown lawyers and certainly in the range of what a doctor makes after paying for their staff and expenses. And this is just paying you for your time; we're not holding inventory and we don't have to manufacture anything. We trade our time and our problem-solving brains for $200 an hour. Who wouldn't want to do more activities that generate that kind of income and less of the activities that pay less than that.

You are not going to make that kind of income filing or chasing down NSF payments or rescheduling a client's appointment several times. That is not an effective use of a busy agents time and talent whose time is worth $200 an hour. NO other professional such as a dentists, lawyers, or CEOs is seen doing that. They outsource tasks that other people are willing to do for $20 an hour and not take the risks of a fluctuating income. Whether you're a manager or agent, do not pay someone (such as yourself) $200 an hour to do filing and booking paramedical orders. Successful businesses just don't work like that.

When you are working—work hard! However, when you are on a family vacation or not able to be effective at work, don't work. It sounds simple but you have permission to turn your brain off once in a while. To ignore this in efforts to make more money can lead to declining health and loss of connection to those important around you. If you're billing at $200 an hour, of course you want as many billable hours as possible but to do that long term you can't be "on" 24/7.

As long as you stay focused, leverage technology to keep unproductive time down to a minimum, outsource the tasks that don't pay you as well, and are efficient in organizing your appointments, you can work eight hours every day and have a possibility of making $1,500 a day. More importantly, you can keep this up for 20 to 30 years without smelling smoke from burnout.

The Difference Between Management and Leadership

Ask yourself, do you feel you are a manager or a leader? However you instinctually answered, you are probably right. If you don't like the answer that is OK, you can change it later if you want to, through sheer force of will.

Many years ago, I was asked to provide a presentation to a group of sales managers about the difference between managers and leaders. I began looking around agencies at managers who conducted themselves as managers who conducted themselves and managers and compared them against those who acted like leaders. The differences were so distinct it made me wonder why I hadn't noticed it before, and that no one else had either.

I have taken some of the common categories that affect the careers of sales managers in our industry and made comparisons based on my own experience and definition.

	Management	Leadership
Career Description	Keeps others accountable for activity and productivity. Seek to be competent and dependable.	Keep yourself accountable to be a role model of a financial professional and leader. Seek to be great
Bisiness Planning	What we do is measured by quarterly reviews to stay in our roles	What we do to enhance our careers
Self-development	Take provided head office courses to be a sales manager	Be a student of the industry and learn from everywhere and everyone. Evolve into a leader in the industry. Go to LAMP and seek designations
Career Path	Follow the timeline and structure of typical career progression	Be creative and distinct; seek opportunities to move through structure faster than peer group.
Teamwork	Don't slow the team down, do your job	Speed the team up, do more than your job
Recruiting	Achieve required number of recruits annually and work backwards in time from that target	Inspire more than enough people to follow you into a new career, select the best
Recruiting activities	Allocate time to find candidates to do aptitude tests, manage their completion	Create opportunities for others to seek you out; COI's, organizations and advisors. Be an expert on 'closing' successful candidates to next meeting
Interviews	Setting agenda for each meeting. Use provided recruiting tools and presentations.	Inspiring others to become excited about a new career. Use intuition and experience to work through objections flawlessly and anticipate competition
Licensing book sales	Have the textbook sign-up forms ready, know details about course, exam dates and resources to assist completing course	Offer guidance and support, tell stories of others before them how they achieved success. Connect and counsel those who fail the exams
Appointing recruits	Coordinating time to appoint that makes sense for candidate and agency	Coordinate timing of agent contracting to align with many 'wins' to give them great launch
Advisor Training	Follow provided textbooks and company content, setting deadlines for material completion. Put agents on basic academic track	Adding stories of how you apply skills, inspire to get requirements done quickly and impress peers. Ask them to be co-presenter at next class.

Joint Field Work	Set activity expectations, pre-brief and debrief appointment. Do pre-contract sales with recruit	Do twice as much post-contract work as pre-contract
Insurance sales	Measure and track sales credits and annual premium, explain their first pay statement	Demonstrate how to leverage sales for more income. Align their goals with campaigns, motivate to show them what is possible
Advisor's World	Know your agency's compensation, products, recognition, process, technology & tools	Know your competitor's compensation, products, recognition, process, technology & tools
Getting agent career off to fast start	Explain the fast-track program, and meet with recruits weekly	Show them your trophy for achieving a fast-start, talk to them daily in first 6 months
Coaching	Open door policy	Go to their office
Perception	Head office thinks we're managers	We think we're leaders
Being 'in' the manager role	Traditional work week setting time aside for lunch	24/7

Essential Priorities for Developing Managers

In any role there are going to be "essential" activities that not only satisfy our expected career duties but, if done well, provide us with success and advancement. The worlds of managers and agents are not that far apart in reality. In fact, I would say the critical components are not as different as either group would position it to be, no matter how much chest thumping occurs over drinks at their company conferences.

Priorities for Agents

- Business plan with calendar (e.g. Valentine's campaign or Critical Illness for Kids' month)
- Prospecting – for insurance, wealth and group benefits clients, asking for referrals
- High Administration – printing quotes, prefilling paperwork, campaign planning
- Low Administration – filing, replying to emails, beneficiary changes and NSFs
- Sales appointments – presenting, needs analysis, closing and objection handling
- Creating Systems and managing staff (remember outsource $15 an hour jobs, you make $200!)
- Professional development – designations, industry magazines, industry conferences
- Marketing – building networks and COIs

Priorities for Managers

- Business plan with calendar (quarterly pace for targets and growth, campaigns, AGM, branch events, training clinics, ethnic holidays)
- Accountability – to head office targets and branch goals

- Prospecting for advisors, managers, and staff; asking for advisor candidate referrals
- High Administration – licensing training, terminations, conflict resolution, compliance
- Low Administration – filing, emails (recommend doing only one hour at beginning and end of each day)
- Interviewing appointments – presenting, selection, closing, and objection handling
- Creating Systems and leverage staff to accomplish goals and run smooth agency
- Professional development – designations, industry magazines, industry conferences, and public speaking
- Marketing – building networking and COIs
- Coaching meetings with under two-year advisors
- Training products, compliance, sales process and licensing, joint fieldwork
- Building agency culture while pursuing the direction agency leadership prescribes

A common question with junior managers, and even established ones, is where they should focus their limited time each day to be effective in their roles (or at least keep their jobs). Some are looking for a composition of an ideal week. For longevity of their success, this is difficult to do depending on what the manager's expected role would be in the organization.

Top manager priorities fall into two main camps: recruiting and production from those new recruits. By themselves, they are two very large tasks but the advantage most new managers have, that experienced ones don't, is that they have accumulated less tasks and distractions that occur throughout each day. They can actually focus, at least during the initial years on these two critical tasks. Let us break them into smaller pieces as well as include items oftentimes required by the organization to be done by the new manager.

Most managers have half of the day to focus on these essential priorities.

Time spent procrastinating, hanging around a colleague's office catching up on the hockey game last night, and golfing are examples of time spent that is largely not required for success, promotion, and income. At the end of the day, whether you have accomplished a key activity to your business or not, that day is over. You can't get it back again or re-do it. A good senior manager will coach and develop their junior managers to be conscious of these precious amounts of time. The junior manager has to accomplish these tasks for the organization and not to accidentally spend time on abstract busyness.

Depending on your particular role in the organization, the sequence of the activities listed may vary but any sales manager in the financial industry will require delivering on most if not all of these points. You may be told that you are primarily a recruiter, a trainer, an office manager, a wealth specialist, and so on but to move forward in your career you would have to be good at ALL these key activities. The same can be said in the military world; whether your specialized role is a medic, artillerymen, or mechanic, when it comes right down to winning the battle, everyone picks up a rifle and joins in the fray. It's the only way to win a game this big.

Prospecting activity is so important that without it none of the other priorities matter. As a sales manager in this industry, if you are not able to identify, communicate with, and attract good quality people in your organization you are not doing your job. What makes an advisor great is to being able to constantly build relationships with many prospects to ensure they have a pool of good potential clients to work with. This is key to survival and prosperity in their careers.

The exact same thing can be said to the sales managers; it is our ability to create and work with a pool of candidates to identify the best people to join our agencies. Success in this arena directly correlates to success in your respective role. Sometimes junior managers limit their prospecting solely for agents and leave the prospecting for staff and managers to the senior managers. What a mistake! There is no reason why junior managers cannot pay attention to all different types of prospects who can benefit their organization.

The easiest way to ensure you get your priorities done is to literally book an appointment with yourself daily or weekly to do essential tasks so enough time is set aside to get the task done. Too often, I see junior managers get busy with training or coaching their advisors only to realize that it is now Wednesday evening and they haven't actually done any recruiting activities. This will usually end in a frenzy of activity for the balance of the week or "writing off" the rest of this week in plans to tackle the task the following week. I believe a junior manager should spend approximately 1/3 of their working week in prospecting for new agents and trust that the remaining 2/3 will fill itself in.

Later in their careers, sales managers can lower this weekly dose of career medicine to 25 percent. Seasoned managers can do this is because they have spent years building COIs, partnering with agents for referrals and refining reliable recruiting sources. Therefore, they are more efficient in being able to identify good candidates without spending a lot of time in diverse and high-effort activities in order to meet people. A junior manager will try ten different prospecting activities to spend an hour with a low caliber candidate over coffee. An experienced manager will have candidates come to the agency office for the meeting. Additionally the interviews held by a senior manager tend to be shorter and more purposeful in nature. It is truly the case of a new manager applying a lot of time and effort to yield the same result as a senior manager who uses their experience to get the same result with less time and effort.

The Home-Work Tight Rope Walk

Tony Defazio

My career path had taken me through the maze of several jobs including an Industrial First Aide attendant, a youth leader, and at age 18, I became a self-employed entrepreneur publishing sports notebooks for coaches. In 1984, I worked as a recreation director at a non-profit organization in Maple Ridge, BC. It was an enjoyable career and very gratifying as I worked with low income and delinquent youths that needed a great deal of guidance and encouragement. That career lasted a good seven years and I thought it was the best job in the world. Unfortunately, working for a non-profit organization means that you probably are not going to be parking a new car in your drive way or purchasing a house in Bel Air with your earnings.

I've never met a fellow agent that grabbed a recruiting brochure and made a decision to become a "life insurance" sales agent. If you are reading this and are a financial planner, insurance agent, or one of many other titles that we identify ourselves with in this industry, you likely were taken out for that free cup of coffee that changed your life. In 1988, I was taken out for that free cup of coffee and 27 years later, I am still enjoying the fruits of my efforts. Although the chain of companies I had worked for included Mutual Life of Canada, which morphed into The Mutual Group then changed to Clarica and then eventually Sun Life Financial, the challenges were the same despite the company insignia: find, keep, and service clients.

My greatest challenge however as a 29-year-old, newly married guy was figuring out how to make a success of the career while finding time to take my wife out on a date once a week and co-parent our four young kids. Probably a dilemma shared by not only our industry but also much of the self-employed world.

I was putting in 40, 50, and even 60 hours a week trying to build a client base to make it work, not untypical of most new recruits in the industry, both then and now. I recall clearly one sunny summer evening looking out my office window and seeing families playing with their kids outside in the park across the street and thinking to myself "what the heck am I doing here being abused by people on the receiving side of my calls who would rather poke themselves in the eye with a cattle prod than have an unsolicited conversation with an insurance agent?" I tried to keep in mind that if I worked really hard for five years I could make the other twenty-five relatively enjoyable. How true this turned out to be.

Allowing a career to devastate your relationships with your spouse or children for me was not an option. I understood a job or career was only a means of simply creating income to sustain the things in life that matter to us. Having a career at the expense of the family, I was taught, leaves one at a place of insignificance.

Fortunately for me, the work/life balance came early as I always tried to have dinner with the family every night and insisted that Friday nights as well as Saturdays and Sundays were off limits for business as were all holidays. Holding to this programme, however, did mean that one had to be very productive during the working days. The evenings were gold for me. Most "mom and pop" prospects worked their normal 9-5 jobs and were available for that dreaded cold calls I was making at that time. Emails, text messaging, and anti-telemarketing regulations were not in play at that time so the evening phone call was pretty much the path to success.

A key attribute to balancing career and family life was to regularly reward oneself with time off—family vacations, planned trips to the park, a game of golf with a friend, or a dinner out with the wife. I always had something to look forward to after getting beat up by cold call monsters and declines by that dreaded underwriter back at head office.

A quote I have held onto over these years was that you start controlling the business or it will control you. How true this turned out to be. This closely matched the discipline we've encouraged our clients to do of saving 10 percent of their paycheque first before anything else. Schedule in a percentage of your time with family, friends, and even your own personal time before committing to all the tasks the career demands. "Paying myself first" was a good work/life balance decision.

Commit to it, schedule it into the workweek, then make all else fit around it. What you find when you do this is that there won't be burnout, and the commonly felt guilt of too much family or too much work will conveniently be balanced. We often spend time at the office being unproductive so when there is a finite amount of time to get the job done, we tend protect work time and family time better.

Much later in my career, I volunteered in many capacities: board member at a Christian school, board member of a local hospice society, hockey and baseball coach, and a Kinsmen member. I had assumed, and feared, these volunteer responsibilities would eat into my work schedule and was going to reduce my production but I found that the very thing I thought was going to pull me from my prospecting actually connected me to other people and prospects. By balancing my time more in the favour of helping others, I was able to drop cold calling and work in the referral-only business!

Over time, our careers continue to reward us with renewals of business. Meeting clients' needs well and taking care of them also provides us the promise that we will eventually work easier to achieve better results.

I now have much more time to dedicate to the family and children, but the children grow up and move on. Had I had the state of mind of growing the career first and getting to the family once I "made it" I would have missed irreplaceable time with family, visits to the hockey rink to watch my son score a goal, and teaching my daughter to ride a bike. Each stage of life only comes once and when you miss the bus, you missed the ride. The most important things in our lives are only things that have the ability to hug back.

By Tony Defazio, CPCA, RHU
27 year agent

Top 10 Do's and Don'ts in my First Year as Sales Manager

	DO	DON'T
1		
2		
3		
4		
5		
6		
7		
8		
9		
10		
	E.g. Job shadow top recruiter	E.g. Spend more than 4 hours/day in office

You know your strengths and weaknesses, your biases and career goals better than anyone. You have also read a lot of material in this book and heard ideas and strategies from some of the best field managers in the business. Now what are going to do, or not do, to have the outstanding sales management career you desire?

Spend a couple minutes to fill out this table. It is OK if you don't get ten right away; you can come back to this book and add more at any time. By thinking about and writing the activities you know deep down you should do, or avoid like the plague, you will have a more accurate compass to steer your career to success.

If you have a senior peer or mentor, it would be a good idea to work on it together or at least show it to them. They will have unique and perhaps more objective insights on you as well as have the experience to give appropriate feedback.

Create a 90 Day plan before starting in Sales Management

WHAT	WHEN	DETAILS
E.g. Have 10 COIs	1 month	Find, meet and select 10 COI's and get 6 month commitment

Whether you are an agent interested in transitioning to sales management, a new manager with the agency, or an established manager wanting to "reboot", creating a focussed 90-day plan can be beneficial. Use some of the ideas you've recently read as a place to start or better yet these ideas might have inspired your own great notions based on your specific role and agency environment.

Like the previous exercise, be as specific as you can, be realistic but also put a little "stretch" in the items you decide will have the most impact for you. This list dovetails well with your organization's quarterly business planning or performance reviews; that's not an accident. However, those documents are for corporate or regional use to measure results that focus on items the company decides is important. This will be your 90-day plan, not theirs! Think about what you want to accomplish at the end of 90 days that will impress you and move you closer to the longer-term career goals you seek.

My 'Bucket List' in a Financial Management Career

WHAT	TIMELINE
E.g. Be a LAMP conference workshop speaker	Within 3 years

When I first started in this industry, I knew I wanted to stretch myself. Looking back at over a dozen years at various levels of management, I have accomplished things I would never have predicted at the beginning. As the years progressed and I achieved targets set for myself, I had to keep moving the bar up in order to keep motivated and stimulated. People often think I'm recognition or income motivated from the way I approach business and competition but that is not true; I'm challenge motivated. Tell me something is next to impossible to do and you have my attention!

What do you want to say you did in this industry before you pack up your office into small cardboard boxes and take your certificates off the wall? The common items I hear from new managers are: a certain income target, qualifying for a prestigious company conference, or being top agency in regional competitions. Don't be limited to what others say should be on your bucket list, they may underestimate what you are actually capable of doing.

There are always bigger mountains to climb, both inside and outside of your current situation. Sometimes it's hard to get excited about your 23rd sales campaign; I get it. Once you have eaten up the conventional challenges in front of you and think you've attained all that there is to win then look farther and further into the future for goals that can take years to achieve. Be creative, use your imagination, and never settle for being above average!

I hope you never run out of mountains to triumph over.

Parting Thoughts

As much as all of us like to personally think our agency could never function or flourish without us, it is simply not the case. We are privileged to have leadership roles within an essential industry but we are only "custodians" of our roles and agencies for a moment in time. My company has been around since the 18th century; it would be arrogant to think I make a huge difference in the overall success of such a large company. I can say, however, that I have impacted the careers of great agents and managers and know giving my best made is pretty good.

Being sales managers, we often get caught up in the seemingly endless stream of critical moments: campaign deadlines, conflicts between agents, getting our 23-page quarterly plan into head office on time, and so on. At the end of the day, I believe long-term success in field management boils down to some pretty basic components:

- Achieving 100 percent of your production goals consistently is better than 140 percent one year only to crash to 74 percent next year. Corporate memories aren't that good; they can quickly forget how awesome you were last year when you look shabby on the reports this year.

- Grow your agency every year, no matter what. Always advance, never retreat.

- Build manager bench strength with strong candidates; you never know when you might need your next manager.

- Develop your craft to be better every year, find a mentor who can give objective feedback.

- Be a member of GAMA and go to LAMP at least once in your career, it's where the best in the business go to share how they do it.

- Identify and develop your successor. Life doesn't wait for you to be ready.

- "Major in the majors"; never forget to focus most of your efforts in what the agency needs to accomplish. This is likely recruiting and

Author Biography

Greg Powell was born and raised in Vancouver, British Columbia and is a graduate of Simon Fraser University with a major in Psychology and minor in Criminology. He was active in a thirteen-year Canadian military career as a Combat Engineer. His duties involved providing leadership during aid-to-civil-power missions such as ice storms, floods, and forest fires as well as participating in international military operations such as the Bosnian War. Greg is a multiple-decorated veteran including the prestigious Governor General of Canada Commendation for his involvement in the Bosnian War, Battle of Medak, in 1993. Greg retired a Sergeant commanding 32 soldiers in 2001 and had a wide range of roles from field operations to military instructor to reconnaissance sergeant.

In 2004, Greg began his career as a financial advisor in the Surrey, BC branch with Clarica, which was one of Canada's largest financial institutions focussing on insurance and investments. Within six months, Greg was selected for the Manager Training Program (MTP) and worked in various positions such as training manager, recruiting manager, and eventually associate manager.

He was later approached for a Regional Manager position that begin in 2007 with the mandate of growth and development within the region. Among many other tasks, Greg collaborated with managers and advisors in the company's transition from Clarica to Sun Life Financial and assisted in the successful rollout of a new management compensation structure. Over 18 months Greg worked with and trained over 400 advisors and 40 managers in BC.

In July of 2008, Greg was offered the position of Financial Centre Manager of the same office he started in as an advisor, and interestingly his father had launched in 1976. Since that time, Greg and his team have achieved regional and national excellence within Sun Life Financial culminating in reaching the President's Circle in 2014, being recognized as one of the top branches for production, agency growth, and advisor quality. He continues to win national industry recognition such as GAMA's "National Management Award," "Agency Builder Award," and the "Agency Achievement Award."

From 2009 to 2012, Greg acted as President of GAMA International Canada, an international association dedicated to developing leaders and managers in the financial services industry. He is a regular contributor to magazines such as *FORUM*, *Money Magazine* and *Advisors Edge*, and a successful public speaker in both Canada and the US. In March 2016 Greg will be speaking at the prestigious LAMP conference in Las Vegas where financial industry leaders from around the world gather to share and learn from the best in the business.

Greg enjoys SCUBA diving, writing, and woodworking. Having travelled by foot across the Arctic Circle, he hopes to travel to Antarctica one day to complete his pole-to-pole experience. In 2010, Greg and his wife Julie Cook, another long-time financial industry manager, travelled to Kazakhstan to adopt their wonderful daughter Lucy. They currently live in Chilliwack, BC.

Speaker Information

Have Greg speak at your AGM or agency conferences this year! Every attendee will receive a signed book as a gift after the presentation!

Connect with Greg

Email:
managersurvivalkit@gmail.com
LinkedIn:
ca.linkedin.com/in/gregpowellatsunlife
Facebook:
www.facebook.com/The-Financial-Managers-Survival-Kit-book-196207350733036/?fref=ts

Book Orders

Books can be purchased online at Amazon.ca, Amazon.com, Amazon.co.uk, Chapters.indigo.ca, BarnesandNoble.com and all good bookstores worldwide.

For bulk orders please contact Lisa@InfluencePublishing.com for special volume discounts.

Would your organization be interested in a personalized version of this book with your company logo printed on the cover? For any orders over 100 books Influence Publishing will add your personalized logo at no extra cost. For personalized branding please email Lisa@InfluencePublishing.com or Tel. 604 980 5700

If you want to get on the path to becoming a published author with
Influence Publishing please go to
www.InfluencePublishing.com

Inspiring books that influence change

More information on our other titles and how to submit your own proposal
can be found at
www.InfluencePublishing.com